WHAT? ME? A TEACHER?

Robert S. Pigott

ISBN\EAN 978-1-257-85121-8

CONTENTS

Born to Run

In my diary I first want to set the stage with the events, people and places that formed my bewildering personality. Maybe I can make it sound as exciting as my sister's. I love reading her diary, probably because it was locked in her drawer for privacy.

Today is the day I've waited four years for, high school graduation. Now I wonder why? Don't get me wrong, I am excited. I just don't really know what to do next. College is so expensive, and the guys get most of the scholarships. So, I'm being forced to enter the workforce. Anyway, I don't want to think about that today.

Today my mother will embarrass me with stories about her rambunctious little girl. I've heard it a hundred times. I used to jump up and down in my crib until it moved to the doorway. That way I could see my Mom or stretch over the crib rail. Sometimes I'd even flip onto the floor and give myself a black eye. Could you blame me? How else could I get outside the door?

Dad will talk about Tojo, our dog. He was the cutest toy poodle. He loved it when I chased him. I think that's what got me running. I guess I was born to run, in lots of ways. Up and down the street and across the yard with large leaps and easy strides Tojo and I would run together as every dog in the neighborhood would bark. Tojo was my best friend, even though my favorite thing was to drop him in the clothes hamper. I'd sit on the lid as he howled and bumped and growled. A couple of times I stuck him in the closet. My Mom would just say, "Thank goodness it was the dog and not her little brother." Tojo's worst fate was to be locked in the closet where no one could hear him whine. Dogs are like that, they love you no matter what.

Now that I think about it, my greatest skill is probably washing the dog. I'm not much for other chores; they just seem to get in the way of life. I guess up until now I haven't been that responsible. I keep promising I will be more grown up when I graduate. But, I'll never outgrow washing the dog. He's fast and fun. He'd zigzag around the house and yard with his near human senses. He didn't want to be caught and tried everything to escape me. I was the only one who could catch the speedster. Sure, I love to take a bath, but not with the dog outdoors in the yard.

Old catalogs were the stage for my dream world allowing me to fulfill my artistic design ambitions by cutting out pictures of women and rearranging their dress with a creative flair. Of course, sometimes I would stumble onto a current catalog with the latest fashions, and I left it with gaping holes. This always thrilled my mother. Since we lived in a rural area the catalog saved time and money, however this was impossible with missing pages. My creative juices were flowing by producing dresses and clothes for my dolls. I spent hours dreaming of new styles, and sometimes demonstrating them on my dog or brothers. Bribing my brothers and sister to dress up and model my creations instilled my ability to manipulate and convince others. This ability proved to be an important future job skill in sales and leadership positions.

I loved to race with the boys in the neighborhood and could beat them with ease. My Dad liked this, but the boys sure didn't! Dad decided to find out just how fast I really was against faster competition by entering the Junior Olympics. First place in my age division built confidence for more competition. I felt sorry for some runners who had trouble running in a straight line. Domination is the best way to describe most of my races in grade school. In high school there were runners who could match my speed so we took advantage of this blessing. Not surprisingly, our four by one hundred relay team set a city record which still stands. This record performance helped remove the tears after we disqualified in a handoff when we were leading in an earlier race. Running also improved my quickness and skills for basketball, and dance team provided agility and a lot of tough competition. What made the sports contests even more intense were the games against my Dad who coached another team. I wanted to get information on how to guard their best player so we can control her and notch up another victory. The seeds of competition and confidence were growing every year as athletics dominated my life.

My mouth has always been one of my serious problems since I lack self control which would result in a defiant and disrespectful attitude. I can only remember using the family car a few times since this was often the punishment. Most of my friends were surprised to know that I was actually able to drive. Teasing and pestering my siblings was one of my favorite pastimes. Often they would hide or turn away when they saw me coming. The usual punishment was no TV and isolation in the bedroom. This was actually a reward, since I could then have complete access to my sister's belongings without any interference. A young girl's most important confidence builder is to have an attractive appearance. Unfortunately, my sister and brothers also wanted to look good, but I was unable to comprehend this. Jumping into the bathroom ahead of my siblings and locking the door was my best strategy. Since we were all on our way to school this created chaos, but what else is new? How was I to know my Dad would take the lock off the door? This calmed the conflict somewhat. When I continued to hold the door shut and not cooperate with time limits he used the ultimate weapon. I could no longer find any of my make up. How could anyone be so cruel to embarrass me at school? Even though I was a slow learner, I did learn how to be considerate of others.

Musical Chairs of Jobs

I am reaching for someone or something as I embrace my diary entries. If I knew my own feelings without questioning everything my life would be a lot easier at home and school. Unfortunately, my grades were not at the level needed for an academic scholarship, and colleges were not yet awarding young women very many athletic incentives. So I decided to work for awhile and save some money (not likely) to buy a car and pay some of my own college costs. Have you ever laid sod on a yard when the temperature is 90 degrees or higher? Lifting the 40 pound rolls of sod onto your shoulder is just the first step. Dirt sifts down your back and even into your pants as you carry the rolled sod on your shoulder and drop it into place on the lawn. And of course the body sweat turns the dirt into mud which sticks to all body parts especially cracks where it itches beyond endurance. I only had to labor for 8 or 10 hours a day, and I forgot to mention, there is also straining and loading the truck between jobs. This is all compounded by muscle aches from the day before, and the lack of a social life as you are too tired to stand let alone run around with friends.

Well maybe it would be easier to work inside at a meat processing plant where it is nice and cool. It sure looks easy to stand there making knife cuts, until you try to do it at the speed of an assembly line. Now, you do have to be careful not to cut off a finger or run a knife through your arm or leg, but at the same time other workers stare and laugh as you fall so far behind. Then, there is the embarrassment of another "knife man" who comes along to bail you out. Where can a "weak sister" hide when there is a pile up of meat which is slowing down the line and costing the company money? If you can avoid cutting a finger off, keep one eye open for incoming meat. In spite of the threat of losing their job, the urge to throw meat pieces is a way to overcome boredom and have fun. It seems some adults never leave their juvenile school days.

Lacking seniority, new workers are frequently moved from job to job. Some jobs defy description. Have you ever tried to eat lunch after working on the gut table? The animal intestines are used for the casings or wrapping of sausage and wieners. The guts need to be cleaned by washing with a hose in large water filled table basins. If the slime and stench is not enough to turn your stomach, consider putting your hands (you can wear gloves) into the water. Swimming near your fingers are tape worms (10 to 15 feet long) and round worms which washed out while cleaning hog intestines. Somehow, lunch just doesn't seem very appealing even if I am hungry. This might be the easy part of the job because somehow you need to adjust to constant ridicule, teasing and harassment by nearby males. They seem to have no skills other than knowing how to communicate offensively with young females. If you have a lot of self discipline and ability to ignore, eventually most of the comments will get old and lose their effect. Where are the assembly line supervisors when you need them?

A quieter place might be in order like a nursing home for the elderly. I always loved my grandparents and these people are too old and decrepit to cause any problems. Don't you agree?

What ever made me think the elderly were quiet and inactive? A 120 pound person is considered a lightweight in comparison to the rest of the population, but have you ever tried to pick them up from a chair and into a bed? It's pretty hard to get a date or anyone to come close to you after spilling a bedpan down your leg and into your shoes. The elderly are often sweet and enjoyable so a person should try to make some friends. However, pleasantly listening to a story three or four times stretches my limits to avoid being rude. One cute older lady spent her time drifting around the halls and eating area pinching various residents and visitors in the butt. Even though they look like my grandparents, I seem to lack the mental discipline to establish myself as a long time and satisfied employee.

If a young man is supposed to go West: why not a young woman? California was supposed to be the land of gold and opportunity. However, getting there is half the battle, and the long drive is only the start of the struggle. We were just cruising along enjoying the sunshine and summer breeze. All of a sudden she was swerving in her car ahead of me. I heard this clunking noise and her car started to growl and jerk. Since my girl friend drove fast and hard it shouldn't have been unexpected when my friend's car broke down. We were soon standing along side the road with strong gusts of wind hitting us from passing trucks. Pushing and crushing, we jammed as much as possible of her belongings into my car. So we left a lot of our possessions along the roadside. –No big deal, doesn't everyone get rich in California? Not only that, in all the confusion many of our personal belongings became lost and mixed up. Therefore, my so called friend wore my clothes and used my toothbrush to clean her shoes. That's not the worst part as I had to leave a large amount of my towels and household necessities to make room for her belongings in my car. At least her Dad drove half way to California to repair her car, but by that time we were long gone into the western sunshine.

It may seem like a low measly job, but I was thrilled to be part of the fashion industry. My job as a fit-model was a good start, but little did I know how expensive it is to live in the Los Angelus area. Living with my employment supervisor for a short time was an unforgettable experience. How would you like to stare your boss in the face every morning before breakfast? Your boss sees you without make up and in your underwear. How can this be good? Try to explain your personal life like telephone arguments with my parents and boyfriend? My future mother-in-law also felt charitable enough to take me into her home, but this was not a sustainable arrangement. Maybe this was a forewarning of what was to happen to my failed marriage. The freedom to set my own destiny was great, but living on the streets did not fulfill the dreams I had made for California. What I thought was a good paying job based on my Midwestern background proved to be an illusion. Paying my share of the rent was like spinning the wheel of fortune since the amount of money available was always a gamble. The food budget was meager, and forget about any other necessities. After my roommate had a minor accident with my car, and loaned it to some foreigners who totally destroyed my only transportation. So the handwriting was on the wall. It was time to go home and look for greener pastures.

Home Sweet Home

Only my diary will understand how I got into the following mess. At least my diary can't talk back and put me down. But, more than anything I need some good advice. Going heavily into debt to finance college and buy another car was a trip to fantasy land. My financial standing was about as solid as a marshmallow. The greener pastures led me to self employment in cosmetics demonstrations and sales. Being proud of my youthful appearance was a confidence builder until reality slapped me in the face. I loved this work, but due to my youthful appearance, it was difficult to convince older home-owners to have a home party. All I wanted was a bumper sticker to show off my success as a top distributor. So why does a person stay locked into a business when sales are moderate to low? If I could answer this question, my whole life would make more sense.

I also found a way to stay physically fit and earn income at the same time. My desire to exercise led me to working part time as an aerobics instructor, and I had connections with a local fitness center in the downtown area. It was a great job which allowed me to have unlimited access to my favorite exercise activity. However, there were a couple of drawbacks. Rarely was there a place to park so I took whatever I could find. Plus, an old car attracts negative attention especially from law enforcement. All of this led to a police car sitting in front of my parent's home broadcasting to the neighborhood for me to come to the door. It was like a Swat team talking to someone holding a hostage. My terrified mother came out on the front porch and tried to figure out what was happening. Since I was at work, my mother had to explain why I had not paid all those parking tickets. Not a very good homecoming by me. It's great to know Moms love a person unconditionally, especially since my Mom sacrificed to keep me going with money and encouragement. Maybe police attention had its benefits of protection of late night money deposits, but I didn't recognize it at the time. My trusting and naive boss gave me all the deposits to drop off at the bank as I was driving home. He must not have known how broke I was, or maybe I just had an innocent face. I was honest and dependable, but carrying large amounts of money down a dark alley late at night is not something a 110 pounder should feel good about. Maybe I should have been teaching martial arts instead of just exercise classes.

I could stay in great physical condition by working out for free, if I could only earn enough to eat and stay alive. I had a multitude of friends as the gym was a busy place for people my age. I enjoyed talking to everyone and this makes me feel accepted and worthwhile. My financial problems are overwhelming, but since I am still single and healthy there is still hope I can turn this around. Nobody said life would be easy, but I am just looking for a life.

Finally—a Future

I know who my best friend is as I make contact with this pen and page to my ever beloved diary. Good grief, the next thing I'll get locked up as a mental case for talking to a book. Speaking of books! College had always been just a dream. Halleluiah for student loans! So what if I had not been in school for years, I still looked five years younger than my age. After all, first impressions are final and I could knock-em dead for the first ten minutes. If the impression took any longer then that it probably isn't worth having anyhow. I was so tired from working it was nice to sit down and listen during classes. I received some credit from previous classes and the four years went so fast. Some strange and deranged people find their way into the world of Art. One instructor keeps flirting and making passes at me. My Dad kept saying I should report him to the administration, but from what we could figure out from other teachers he was a born troublemaker. Maybe I was too sensitive for the world of Art. It was about the fifth class, and we were studying how to draw human anatomy. How was I supposed to know he was going to take all his clothes off? A model was invited and when he got down to his underwear I was ready to leave. It's really hard to draw a human form with your eyes closed. At least I had the nerve to stay for the entire class. A friend of mine faked sickness to leave the room and never did return to class.

It was a rewarding experience to promote and participate in my own Art shows and I began to feel confident about a rewarding career as Graphics

Arts major. After graduating from college, the world seemed to be calling me to seek my place in the world. Even though I participated in contests in which our team won advertising awards the economy was weak, and jobs were limited in my chosen field. What could be more exciting adventure than working for an airline? All this excitement meant cleaning waste disposal from toilets and struggling to carry and load luggage which weighed more than me. Tossing and rearranging baggage in the dark recesses of the cargo area was like visiting the house of horrors on Halloween. I worked in a small but busy airline terminal, and it was always interesting to see and talk with travelers. Late night hours were especially exciting and adventuresome since there were often hours alone in areas of the terminal where few could be summoned for help. After work, the parking lot was like a dark auditorium after everyone had gone home. Since I came later in the day my car was in the farthest, lightless corner of the parking lot. Yes, I am afraid of the dark and a lot of other scary places.

One of my favorite memories was of a guy who did not know which end he was standing on. He was a born comic, and a lot of fun to work with. Airlines are strict about appearance and being overweight was a cardinal sin. Well, he was just two pounds over his weight requirement, and he didn't want this correction on his evaluation. Since he could not talk his way out of the problem fast action was needed. Just as he was about to be written up for excess weight he hollered, "Hold everything." He then began to undress in front of everyone throwing his clothes all over the place. He made weight! That was just one sample of what he as capable of doing. He was also my assigned partner to de-ice aircraft during ice storms. We had these large hoses with a lot of pressure and used them to spray the aircraft wings so ice would not cause a drag. The ladder must have been 20 feet high and I couldn't hold on to the hose with the wind and pressure. As always, he would climb the ladder and complaining he always had to "bail-out" the female workers. I think he really liked being around us, and looked for opportunities to provide assistance. He always seemed to be the one conveniently available when we had heavy lifting to be done loading baggage.

However, persistence does pay off and my promotion to the counter greeting customers sure beats hernia surgery from lifting large luggage. However, the human element can prove to be more difficult than any physical labor. How do you console a customer who came an hour and half early just to stand in line behind someone who needs a lot of attention and service? Neither person could understand why everything was delayed. Or, when an angry frequent traveler who knows the luggage and personal inspection routine blindfolded is still delayed. The line seems without end with a large number of families who are unorganized and confused by it all. My customer service skills were reduced to childish whining. I repeat over and over to myself, "keep your eye on the prize of reducing the anger and invite them to travel again."

Why shouldn't I look for a new position everyone else tries to move up? What could be better than an instructor on airline procedures and customer care? Somehow, I was selected and the only reason must be my attitude of a teacher. What a great opportunity-I think! All my highly motivated students are airline employees who need their jobs. Why shouldn't they want to learn the material so they have excellent evaluations? It sure sounds logical, but somehow human nature has a contrary nature to it especially if we don't understand or see the need for the training. The general attitude is, this has nothing to do with my job performance or duties, and I resent being forced to be here when I could be doing something more productive. Since when does maturity of young adults really mean anything? Instead of concerns about job retention and security students are late to class, and continually talk without paying attention to the presentation. And worst of all I'm ridiculed as a "gung ho" type or company person. So apparently teacher authority is non-existent even when the paycheck is on the line.

How exciting, somehow I was selected to fill an airline flight attendant position in Phoenix. Once again I headed west to seek my fortune. Say another prayer as; my older car will be tested to its limits. Since when would I allow a small problem of transportation stand in my way? The apple doesn't fall far from the tree when it comes to my bull headedness. My Dad and I took turns to drive straight through in a 33 hour odyssey. It was a weekend and we left late Friday afternoon, and he booked a flight back on Sunday afternoon so he could return to work. I have been called a Pollyanna because only fun and exciting things happen to me. Maybe it's because I love new challenges and danger is very attractive to me. One scary incident happened when we stopped for gas in New Mexico. A number of rowdy and loud drunks were yelling and roaming around the gas station. Dad kept demanding I should stay in the car, but since when have I listened to anyone?

When a drunk yelled and staggered toward me, once again my lighting fast running ability saved the night. Dad was behind the wheel and it was probably the first time he spinned the wheels leaving anywhere. It was just like a drag race.

However, most of the time it was nothing but endless pavement, and body soreness from sitting in one position. What I would give for a short workout or a fast dance. There were a few worries about the car overheating, but the real challenge was staying awake. We really could not sleep very long due to worrying about the other driver dozing off. The landscape and trees were awesome as we descended from the Grand Canyon area.

A few hours North of Phoenix my attention had deteriorated to a zombie like condition. Driving only 45 mph was not going to get us there on time so my Dad had to drive a double shift. After several hours with nothing but on-coming headlights the bright neon lights of Phoenix startled and stimulated our brains. It's a much drier climate and the wind blows the fine sand into your hair and sticks to your skin especially after walking through a mist cooling spray. Late at night the traffic was still heavy, and we were able to follow directions to the apartment in spite of exhaustion.

My blurry eyed Dad tried to sleep for a short time before heading to the airport for the return flight. What are the chances? From the heavens above of out of control noise pounding down from above! All he wanted was a few hours sleep. The apartment above us was having a wild and loud party, but my Dad was so tired his senses seemed to be dead. We got him to my favorite work place and with a little help he was off to the wild blue yonder and a little peace and quiet. I was able to room with a long time friend who was always a lot of fun. Never a dull moment so we were a good match for just about anything. Cheryl could drive any store clerk crazy in five minutes and all my worries faded away around her. She is best remembered in my family for "borrowing" a pair of my brother's shorts when he was gone. He ran into her as he came home from football practice tired and impatient. She was somewhat overbearing and actually paraded in front of him down the driveway enjoying his seething anger.

However, hope reigns eternal, and my next opportunity will come when I was accepted as a flight attendant both domestic and international. Domestic flights test your ability to sleep, like swing shift workers you lose track of day and night, and your body rhythms are drastically altered. My lifestyle resembled the mad hatter's charge in multiple directions as shopping, appointments and visiting friends became a confusing nightmare. Air travel is a confirmed duty of most business operations and family travel, so a flight attendant had better be capable of soothing the irritated egos. When they say jump, you say, how high?

International charter flights are a different story depending on where the spinning wheel of scheduling and volunteering comes to rest. Trips to Ireland were fun and delightful as visits were made to my ancestral towns and villages. The people were fun loving and friendly asking about my Irish heritage. What could be more fun than an invitation to visit an Irish pub and farm store bearing my surname? Germany, also the home of my mother's ancestors, was exciting with many historical sites to visit. I'm not sure whether I like being German or Irish heritage. Not much chance of changing my genes anyway. Which country is the most fun loving? We also had to transport U.S. military forces to various locations including Middle Eastern countries. It was an experience I will never forget. Few people realize the indignities our military personnel must endure when serving in foreign lands of the Middle East. Our bravest defenders, who daily risk their lives, are not allowed to bring bibles or Christian religious possessions into countries they are protecting. The flight attendants also are subject to these rules and regulations, and are often required to relinquish their passports. So much fear has been injected into these Middle East stopovers when transporting troops, some flight attendants sleep six to a room in order to feel secure from possible harassment. A male is allowed to slap a woman, other than his wife, if she speaks to him in public. So much for equal rights and respect for free speech.

Speaking of violence! Most of the flights were long and boring, but I couldn't sleep after this incident. We were about to take off from a Florida stop over, and I told this guy he would have to take his seat. Also, the bag he was carrying would have to be placed under the seat or overhead compartments. His reply was "I can't since I have a bomb inside." Well, I knew my duty was to tell the captain, but as I turned around he said "Don't leave; I have a gun in my pocket." One of the other flight attendants noticed what was happening and informed the captain. By this time the slurred speech and glassy eyes told me this guy was drunk. Never the less airport security and the FBI were on the scene and the European sports reporter was removed. Actually, he had just covered a large soccer competition which was his last for that employment.

Another flight was even more shocking since it involved the basic human right to life. Unforgettable experiences have been the rule of my life, but the trip to China was beyond belief for most Americans. A large group of refugees had crossed the Pacific from China, and instead of landing in the United States ocean currents pushed them into Central America. As a result, they could not apply for asylum in the United States, and were to be deported from Central America. A questionable humanitarian charter flight was provided by the U.S. to return the freedom seekers to China. After a rather harrowing landing to avoid nearby buildings, and a hazardous steep descent we landed safely. The refugees were marched across the airfield as many speculated their fate. A dictatorial country, China has a long history of treating dissent with cruelty including death squads. Many believe the refugees, who were only fleeing to seek freedom, meant their destiny with a firing squad. Some say it is a money making enterprise since young body parts can then be sold on the international market for exorbitant prices. Not all flights are visits to a tropical paradise.

China is a place full of surprises and the unexpected. With two female friends, the enticement of bargain shopping for unique clothes was an irresistible offer. The older aging man did not seem to offer any threat or danger. We were soon winding our way down cluttered alleys with lots of turns and darkness. At this point anyone with common sense would have turned and ran away. Basically, we had no clue which way to run, and totally at the mercy of the little old man.

Suddenly, we went through a narrow door which opened into a large room full of smoking and seedy looking men. Was this a human slavery operation? Just as we were about to turn and try to run a familiar voice told us to follow him. An airline security guard had seen us turn into the alley and thank God he continued to follow us. As the security guard followed us providing directions, he also lambasted us with a lecture on safety. Normally, one of us would have had a smart comment about being old enough to take care of ourselves. Humility and fear seemed to be the top priority virtues at this time.

Speaking of paradise, I thought I had found it in a young man who appeared to have everything I was looking for. Actually, he had a lot more than I was looking for, and my parents seemed to recognize this. My parents traveled to Phoenix in order to manage, pay for and watch the wedding with reluctant concern. They had religious and character based questions about my singer/missionary. It was a Jewish style wedding as I wanted a biblical connection even though no one seemed to have any Jewish heritage. After preparing all the food, taking care of announcements, helping with my dress another ominous message was sent from up above. What else could it be, knowing the weather history of Phoenix? My plans were for an outdoor wedding in a park, and the weather channel said it had been nearly a century since it had rained heavily this time of year. It wasn't just a rain shower, but deluge of biblical proportions. Sure enough, everything we had prepared had to be moved inside to a church. My life has always been chaos, but nothing like this. We had no idea where to arrange seating, the trellis, food service and participants. It was like trying to control a run-away freight train, and I was oblivious as to what I was actually getting into. The wedding was actually the easy part.

When you work hard and put forth extra effort by volunteering for flights most flight attendants do not want the reward which is more "opportunities" or assignments. What would be the best gift was a few days of rest, and we were about to get it. This is what most of us want to believe, but then reality jumps up and kicks us in the face. The years of dedication to lifting heavy cargo, sleepless nights and abusive travelers is about to end with a layoff. Should you stick around and hope for a recall or move on to even more misery? In addition to all this, I need to consider my newly acquired husband. He had handsome appearance, nice personality, music ability, aspiration for Christian missionary work and a drug habit. What do you do, when under the influence; he puts your cat in the microwave? He blew my $5000. severance pay on drugs and clogged the toilet with needles. And that's just the minor stuff.

A Run for Freedom

I'm sure glad my diary is a private place telling another person about this experience is beyond embarrassment. My honeymoon was supposed to last forever! How about a couple of months? My dream world is turning into a nightmare. Since my husband can not hold a steady or good paying job there is only one choice, and that would be to use my sales ability in the wholesale and retail women's' clothing business. Did I tell you how I got to Dallas? My sister and her husband decided to perform their charitable duty by renting a truck and driving me and my possessions out of Phoenix. How was I supposed to know the truck did not have air conditioning? My cat was stressed to the max by heat and truck noise that she lost massive amounts of hair. Have you ever tried to eat a hair sandwich? How do you remove hair after it sticks to sweat? After hours of bouncing around against each other in the cab, Dallas seemed like heaven on the horizon. I'm still not sure why my sister allowed me to live with her after the suffering ride from Phoenix.

My first effort was to travel a large circuit around the Dallas, TX region promoting, displaying and placing clothes. I am still in love with clothing and the fashion business. My sister set me up with a clothing wholesaler who had a sales position calling on area retailers. A very hot job when your decrepit vehicle does not have air conditioning and your make up runs down your face from sweat. First impressions are final, and my prospects must have wondered if I traveled on a motorcycle. But the good news, sales have proved me to be very capable and successful. However, the husband left behind is now looking for a handout, and I need to make tracks for greener pastures. What makes him think I have enough money to even survive, let alone support a drug habit?

My Dad says my great-grandmother's family has been traced to the Randolphs of Virginia, and here I am. Virginia was the home of long time friends who were very successful. The economy is good, and my new adventure has landed a job indoors at retail clothing store. My love of clothes, and experience in the field resulted in success as the top producer in the entire region. Every time a store was down in sales, here comes the-super salesperson to the rescue. At least I impressed a lot of the area management transferring from store to store.

I still can't believe he found me! Who told him I was in Virginia? It's like getting rid of a stray dog once you feed him. If his physical and mental abuse was not enough just being around him was extremely dangerous. All he wanted to do was to talk, so it probably would not hurt to ride with him. It was hard to tell if he was using. His emotional tirades whether under the influence or not were unbearable. Maybe this was a dumb thing to do, but I squirmed into the front seat. After ranting and driving recklessly he would not let me out of the car. It seemed like hours of terror and the police must not patrol this area. Being trapped with a mentally deranged drug user is no way to spend a relaxing Saturday evening. After he tried to drive off an interstate bridge I decided staying in the car would be my second bad decision. When rounding a corner, I saw my chance, and opened the door and jumped out at 40mph. Maybe it was all the exercise and athletic ability, but somehow the worst damage was a lot of cuts and bruises. Eventually, the divorce came through and a return to Dallas opened an opportunity for wholesale clothing sales and part time work as a waitress. The customers were upper class and tips were good. People are fun and interesting which draws me into frequent and friendly conversations. How was I to know that Ross Perot came in for coffee everyday? It was sure nice of him to talk to me, and the autograph of a former Presidential candidate was a nice gift to my to my Dad who teaches and follows politics.

Never for a minute was there any thought of remarrying so quickly, and who wants to operate an entire restaurant business? I was swept off my feet, and saying yes once again to a marriage proposal. I had known him since high school, and he was so persistent. Perhaps it was the loneliness, but it seemed like the only future I could count on, and I love adventure. We moved to the heartland of the upper Midwest to operate his passion - a restaurant. For the next few years there were a series of successful and not very successful businesses. It was fun visiting with customers and making friends. The downtown locations brought in a lot of business type customers, and I made friends with people who actually came to the restaurant as a second home. We had the largest and best tasting burritos in the Midwest. Remodeling the interior and decorating to attract customers was something I was born to do. Enjoying friendships with customers is like having a large family, but you don't have the conflicts of living with them. A few customers ran in races against my Dad so my coaching strategy was to encourage more food to slow them down. I love the excitement of the downtown business community and all the parades, art shows, and constant activity. There is something about teenagers and young people to add freshness and excitement to a business. After all, I am fixated as a teenager myself and I love it. This group of young students was looking for exposure for their band, and they brought stimulation, color and friendliness with their music. Good food is not the only thing that attracts customers.

Even though I complain about my knees, staying physically fit is a life time goal. Somehow I drifted into a physical fitness center, and as fate directs my life I was able to find part time work as an aerobics instructor. It's a great way to keep my weight down and the dance music gave me a much needed attitude uplift. I am my own worst enemy for keeping my life stressed and over committed. Working at the restaurant took most of my energy, but I found something even better. I was blessed to teach an art class with a large but wonderful group of children. My Dad often said finding a job you loved means you will never have to work again. What could be better than working with children? This has to be a foreshadowing for future career.

It was desperately inconvenient sleeping and living in the back room of the restaurant. Yet, it sure beats sleeping on the streets. Our bed was on a raised floor in the dark, scary rear of the building. Jumping out of bed or a walking nightmare would result in a concussion on the low ceiling. Actually, an old sink can serve as a bathtub, if you have the legs like a pretzel. No clean place to hang my clothes. To my revelation, this was certainly not a way to reflect and express my fashion talent. The smell of the kitchen can be comforting, but after twenty four hours it becomes sickening. The "boss" had definite guidelines as to the operation of the business so everyone had to learn fast and work hard at all times. He was right about one thing; most of the customers come about the same time and want their food immediately. The speed and quality of service are the make or break elements of this business. We did have a secret recipe for a burrito made from his grandmother's cookbook. People sure seemed to enjoy the taste, and we needed every edge we could get. Money was always difficult to come by, and it contributed to strong differences of priorities on how it should be spent. There were struggles and major differences in this marriage, but usually the rough spots were ironed out.

Since money was in short supply all new opportunities were given a watchful eye. Creativity was a definite asset in this household of an artist and a food connoisseur. Our tasty new taco was widely well accepted and had the potential to be a financial and popular new product for the masses. This idea could have changed our lives, but even the best products require extensive financial investment for marketing and promotion. Unless you are very lucky to receive widespread exposure the delicious new taco will be relegated to just a few fortunate restaurants.

A person can't sit around and cry in their beer when the business requires a move due to rental differences with the landlord. Our relocation to a new building changes the customer base and creates other expenses. In other words, we could not make ends meet. Maybe it was time for a total change of direction. After all I had been constant chaos all my life. What's one more change? The financial decision was to find a more steady income. The next adventure will be "on the road." What the heck is an 18 wheeler? A truck driving school in Tennessee has the program to instill the skills that few men and almost no women possess. Consider the fact all my experience was on small compact cars that rarely ran reliably. Nervous is too mild a word to describe my shaking and lack of confidence. Maybe it was all my aerobics and athletics, but I was at the top of the class in just about everything. Ever try to back up an 18 wheeler into a narrow loading dock? Can you gauge how close you are to the weight capacity of a- decrepit bridge? How about figuring how far you can swing into an intersection without hitting a turning car or the curb? The instructor kept pushing me to drive faster, but all I could see was my ex-husband going off a bridge.

What is it like to feel the massive bulk of semi-tractor trailer as you sit above the traffic like a lumbering elephant, and shaking like a runaway roller coaster? Learn to adjust your visual perspective when passing a vehicle in order to develop the correct distance to return to your lane without running the passed vehicle into the ditch. That maneuver is easy compared to backing into a loading area using your mirrors to adjust turns and not damage the equipment. Then there is the equipment which must be checked periodically so the brakes will hold, the load is secure, and tires are safe. If that was all that could go wrong driving would be a piece of cake. Have you ever pulled an all nighter and then recover your need for rest and sleep in the back of the cab? Traveling on the road has the comfort of riding a horse. Sleep becomes a low priority since making delivery deadlines determine how many future jobs you will be assigned.

Perhaps stress, chaos and frustration could have been solved with a global positioning system, but this was not part of the tractor equipment. If you have ever been to a large metropolitan area just knowing which interstate exit to take can be a difficult task, and you still have to locate and drive to the warehouse or destination to unload. What if you turn down a narrow street only to see a bridge which will not support your weight? Do you back up hoping to find a cross street wide enough to back into and turn around? Or do you take a chance and go over the bridge knowing you could lose your tractor-trailer, load, life and of course collapse the bridge? Even a GPS could not solve this problem. Since you must meet the delivery deadline, rest and personal needs are secondary. So what if you haven't had a shower in a week? You can always call home to seek comfort from the voices of your parents. It must be a carry over from childhood! Just because you are sitting at a truck stop in the darkness and you have no idea where you are is no reason to give up or panic. But you must cry if for no other reason than to relieve stress and receive sympathy from your parents. Driving the massive tractor-trailer is well within my confidence and ability, but what about the dirt, grim, sweat and lack of clean clothes? I just want to be a girl again, to fix my hair, shower and put on make-up!

Six months behind the wheel is enough, and I need to go home. Wherever that is! Not only have we lost track of time, but being absent from our apartment for six months has created a nightmare. As usual we were short financially and we have another problem. The landlady is threatening to throw all our furniture and personal belongings into the street for non-payment of the rent. Maybe my parents could put our belongings in the living room of their small house if they can lift, carry and load it. You guessed it-they stumbled over my belongings for about four months. Abandoning a husband out on the road is not a good idea, but neither is turning into a tramp. Taking a permanent leave of absence was my break for freedom and a stable existence. Now I will have to spend the next three months living with my parents in that small house, and listening to my Dad lecture about wrong decisions.

I Love Teaching

It's a good thing a diary can't talk back because the first words I would hear are "not again!" The stars are bright deep in the heart of Texas since I can now see an opportunity. What will my diary think of this? Finally, the lone star of Texas called again and answered my long desire and frustrating quest to be a teacher. Impossible dream since the courses to earn teacher certification cost $15,000. It was only my annual income, why should this be a problem? I needed a State like Texas that had a severe shortage and recruited teachers. The fact that Dallas has huge population growth has required the educational system to provide fast track teacher certification programs. Working and attending classes has been my life, and the low cost of tuition would still allow us to eat.

The 800 mile trip to Dallas would be an adventure since my parents and cats were coming along. The last time I traveled with my cats they lost a lot of fur due to stress. The taste, itch and floating site of cat fur was an unforgettable experience. Driving a straight truck with all our possessions was easier than a semi, but I still had the cats. As much as I love my cats their fur flying around and cleaning up feces inside the cab is more than even an animal lover can tolerate. The long and tiring drive almost ended in disaster as we came up over a bridge and a fire truck was blocking two of the three lanes. Swerving to the left following my Dad, we just missed this emergency vehicle which had no warning posted before the bridge. My career was nearly over before it started. We then drove to the darkest, isolated, difficult to locate truck terminal in Dallas to pick up my husband. The next day, my Dad risked a hernia unloading the truck with the assistance of my newly acquired pastor and an over-friendly young man from a near-by apartment.

My teaching position was available immediately as the school agreed to a temporary teaching certificate. This arrangement involved taking qualifying courses over the next few years. Recognition for my artistic ability at college art shows was enjoyable, but sharing success with students was even better. We were involved in art projects in several communities. However, what I did not realize was my aptitude to guide and inspire student artists. The responsibility and personal commitment was intimidating. As awards and success accumulated, I realized how good it felt to assist students. Youngsters are so enthusiastic and excited about personal achievement and recognition, and we had more than our share of Art awards. Standing with the Governor to receive awards certainly builds confidence for additional entries. The number of art contests and awards became a monthly occurrence. It was a perfect match of my enthusiasm combined with students wanting and needing attention.

There is nothing in life that realistically prepares a person for your first year of teaching elementary and secondary students. Depending on how many years have passed since you graduated from High School your memories are irrationally distorted in regard to the student-teacher relationship. Unfortunately, you probably remember a few incidents from High School, and the elementary years are fragmented and distorted. However, this is the mindset used as a reference as to how you will interact with students.

Most teachers also use experiences as a model for setting the classroom climate. What most fail to realize is the fact that as society changes so does the student population and attitudes. It may seem contradictory, but in spite of societal changes the basic needs of love, respect and recognition are still present and form the basis for positive relationships. Many new teachers enter the classroom with misperceptions confusing age maturity, and applying memories of their own experiences to the new situation. It often takes almost two years of trial and error to develop the correct language habits and feel comfortable with your own teaching style. Knowing all of this made little or no difference since experiencing the process is the only way to understand and accept the necessary changes. I did have an advantage since my Dad had spent 37 years teaching, and I could rely on his experience and advice. Talk about being in the dark in the classroom. He told me of a great day he was having with students' attention and a smooth presentation. Suddenly, it was so dark he couldn't see his hand in front of his face. He was assigned an inside the hall windowless room, and the emergency lights did not engage. In the back of the room a young man, who was seated in a far corner for disciplinary reasons, struck his cigarette lighter. That's all we need he said to himself, a fire with no idea where to exit. Usually, there was some light coming from windows in other classroom, but not this time. So the only thing he could come up with was "never fear, your teacher's here." Not much consolation to self reliant and over active ninth graders. They eventually had to fumble their way out into the main hallway, and the principal walked around dismissing school. For all you animal lovers, a squirrel had climbed a utility pole and chewed its way into a transformer which short circuited the entire area.

Where do I Start?

Instead of keeping a diary I have decided to make a new beginning by overcoming my tendency to be private. Why shouldn't I share my mistakes, grief and learning experiences with others? Especially confiding with other teachers? From now on I am creating a journal so I can remind myself of important-attitudes and techniques that make a teacher's life rewarding. Who knows, maybe someone will inherit or find this journal so they can learn from my mistakes? Do I have advice for teachers? Well, does a duck like water?

Usually, there are two or three days prior to the arrival of students in which a person attends meetings, in-service programs and organizes the classroom. Learning to use this time makes opening days easier. My problem is wasting the opportunity on socializing with my many friends. After all, I have to set some priorities! They are my support, and year after year I have created an addiction to them. In order to compensate, I have to arrive early which is a good time to accomplish a lot without interruptions. The Principal appreciates extra effort and it is very important to establish a favorable relationship because this is the person doing teacher evaluations. Certainly, a positive relationship will build confidence in both of us. There are probably going to be a few complaints, and if the Principal knows my attitude and personality they should be able to address issues from a position of confidence rather than intimidation. The Principal also assigns extra duties and class assignments so a positive friendship has additional fringe benefits. What are some of the motivational and essential tasks that need attention? Preparing for student arrival makes me enthusiastic and positive. I can't remember feeling this excited when returning as a student. My highest priority was seeing my classmates again. I found out the hard way at the airline that the teacher sets the climate not the students. Being a rookie is difficult, but since I learned a lesson my life will be better. Positive motivation is important on the job and in the classroom will provide dividends for both teacher and students. Let's take care of the visual first since being a woman I certainly know how important appearance can be. What is going to make a student's eyes pop out and think about their future? A trip to a teacher supply store to pick up some postures, decorations and new ideas will help me create unforgettable impressions and motivations. The atmosphere will set a theme and brighten attitudes. I always try to save some colorful and eye catching magazine pictures and calendars. This will add uniqueness to the classroom. When older students move on to another building I can use some of the best images a second time.

Motivation is half the battle so the classroom appearance should reflect this theme. Jumping into the lesson without adequate preparation is like hitting an unsuspecting person with a baseball bat. I learned the hard way, through student laughter and ridicule. My introduction is to plan and establish interest in subject areas with a five minute motivational presentation for each new lesson. Also, I need to reinforce the goals periodically. It is necessary to validate the reason we are putting in the time and effort on each subject, and how success will contribute to job and life skills. A handout explaining class goals, including respect for each other, is another important task.

What else is important? Just as soon as the class lists are available consult last year's teachers to learn name pronunciations and any personal behaviors a student has demonstrated. Some students have special talents like computer or art which can give them extra credit, create student ownership and contribute too many class projects. Not only do you need to know the students, but there are always new teachers. If a person was absent from or not paying attention at the faculty meeting you could embarrass yourself. At the first all classes' assembly my seat was on the outside row-which assisted quick access to students for any number of reasons. Teachers are well aware that students need to remain seated at assemblies and not chase around after friends. That's why I confronted a young person heading up the aisle by asking why she had the audacity to be out of her seat. She quickly informed me that as new teacher she was checking attendance. So much for a good start to the school year and teacher camaraderie. Be prepared to have names added as students return late from vacation or just refuse to come the first few days. It can be irritating but we are still legally responsible to report their attendance.

Nothing is more embarrassing than not having enough books so the student either feels left out or worse. That he or she does not have to start working until they receive a book. This reminds me of a story my grandfather used to tell about not being able to afford the 25 cent book rental during the Great Depression. He had to take the course without a book. So count your students and have three or four extra copies for unexpected arrivals. I remind myself to count desks so no one has to stand at the back of the room or sit on the floor. I have enough unforeseen problems without creating difficulties for students and teacher by establishing an atmosphere of disorganization and unpreparedness. Sometimes a seating chart is helpful especially if it is a large class since it shows the teacher is well organized.

Some teachers don't want to make changes as new students arrive, but what is the alternative? Total chaos? I discovered that allowing students to select their own seats depends on their maturity. I always keep a close watch for undersized student desks since it is hard enough to sit still even when you are comfortable. Try sitting in one of those uncomfortable desks. How long it takes before a person starts to squirm and feel tortured? Now a teacher will know when they have talked too long. It might help avoid being impatient when students squirm around. Some desks are missing gliders and support for the frame. Ever try writing when your desk is wiggling? I remind myself to ask if there are vision or other physical problems so a person can make immediate adjustments. Sometime in the first few days names need to be entered into a grade book or computer. I must review how to report class attendance due to legal responsibilities and to avoid embarrassment when student inquiries arrive.

Should books be distributed the first day? Well, it provides students an opportunity to read ahead and develop an interest in the material, and sets the stage for working on assignments. Occasionally, a student will lose a book like I did, and be afraid to ask for another one. Some system is needed to identify who has each book in the event they are mixed up, lost or stolen so there is a way to determine responsibility. Electronic scanners sure would be nice. I count my students and have three or four extra copies for unexpected arrivals. Some teachers have students complete a voluntary information sheet to have up to date addresses and telephone numbers. I ask for optional health information for emergencies and for hobbies and school activities to develop relationships. Is it important to have a seating arrangement? Some advantages are learning students' names, noting nicknames, providing vision and hearing accommodations, separating problem behaviors and taking role outside during emergency situations.

Taking the time to learn correct name pronunciation pays dividends since many names are very different than the obvious spelling. You can mispronounce a couple of times, but after that grace period students become annoyed and make emphatic corrections. Sometimes it helps to write the syllable sounds of the name in your seating chart for quick reference. No matter how hard you try we can develop a mental block especially if we have similar appearing siblings. I once told a young lady if I called her by her sister's name again, she could come up and kick me in the shins. Thank goodness she was a considerate person or I would have been limping most of the day. It was a soft kick.

How do you address a young man from Southeast Asia with a last name of 19 letters which I never could pronounce? Then there are the situations in which you have three students with the same name. Even when they are strategically placed so you have to look to difference parts of the room, eventually two people will answer at once so I just try to make a diplomatic selection. Talk about seat placement and appearances consider the following situation. I'll never forget the young man who struck terror in my heart when he entered at over six feet tall, unshaven with large sideburns and a black leather jacket. Very few students ever ask to sit in the front row, and these guys gravitate toward the back of the room. I was wondering how anyone could see around his large head and shoulders. Even though his name was John he wanted to be called Elvis. Later, it all made sense as he was in love with the King of Rock. I was expecting a rowdy troublemaker, but his behavior was a model of respect for all students.

I have been told attendance is not just a minor detail presented to parents on report cards. If a student has been absent and the teacher fails to notify the office it can be a legal liability in regard to the child's safety. A young man who had gifted ability and was able to skip a grade is an example of the need for accurate records. He had a history of flashing gang signs, selling his Ritalin to eager buyers, and threatened lawsuits by his mother for failure to meet his needs. He was often sent to the office for tardiness and class disruption, and would delay his return to class. After an unusually long absence I broke a rule which is almost impossible to maintain without exception. I left my classroom exposing me to liability for disasters of unsupervised students. It would be nice to think the teacher next door could actually look in and control any problems. This happens only in a perfect dream world. Teachers are still liable. In the hallway I asked one of the custodians and he mentioned hearing a noise in the auditorium.

When investigating he was drawn to the stage, and hearing a noise he looked up. There was my student climbing the scaffolding forty feet in the air. The student was seeking a hiding spot, probably to skip class and brag to his friends. Regardless, of his disobedience he was still my responsibility along with the principal.

Keeping accurate records of attendance and tardies can and will come back to haunt a teacher. I give special attention to those students who come late when I'm really busy. It is easy to forget to change the attendance and occasionally school officials will inquire about records if the student is trying to avoid an accusation. A young man, who was released from a juvenile prison, was the first and only student to call me an obscene name. He was quiet most of the time, but his attendance was erratic. The school police officer and a backup officer came to my classroom door and requested to see this young man. As the student left, I thought he might be gone for several days so I followed him out to talk about attendance. He was spread eagle against the wall being searched, and when I mentioned attendance the Officer said, "He won't be back."

Also, students can be excused from test requirements, like final exams, by not accumulating absences or tardies. To some students not taking a final test is more important than the class grade. Now, Mom and Dad and the principal are all involved so my attendance had better be accurate. To add to the confusion, some absences are excused and the criteria for this are not only confusing, but subject to interpretation. We teachers wish each other luck with attendance standards and records as they are going to need it.

Now its time to construct lesson plans which will probably be revised as unexpected assemblies, meetings or weather changes everything. Ask a teacher what they least can afford to lose other than their mind. Often it is lesson plans especially if they are detailed and required to be submitted to the boss. It can be grueling to allocate the correct amount of time, but without plans chaos becomes the agenda. Reading bulletins and listening carefully to all announcements will make my life easier since a missed schedule change leaves lesson plans worthless. It is beyond embarrassment to rely on students for updates on meetings, assemblies and weather related dismissals. In other words, accurate information comes from listening to and reading faculty announcements.-Ever fail to attend or come late to a meeting because you did not make note of the time and place? I would rather streak naked at a football game then come late to a meeting again or be caught unaware of an early dismissal. All I could do was stand there and look dumb.

The first two weeks set the stage for relationships between students and teacher. After this period of forming impressions and making emotional connections, I can now relax. The first impressions stage of evaluation is over and we all hope that first impressions are not final. Now everyone can be more honest and allow our real personalities to surface. It's a good time since no one seems to be tired of attending, and with a few exceptions no serious problems have emerged. Self discipline is one of the greatest battles in life so it's time to see if I have actually developed any of this. I need to remind myself of the general attitude I want to project, and form a habit of maintaining my persona in the event of a behavior problem.

What is the most important teacher quality and self discipline? Nothing will happen unless you prepare, prepare and then prepare some more. The good news is preparation will help your confidence when presenting lessons and students will accept your leadership. However, the bad news is preparation never ends. I would probably expect to spend the day prior to classes reading and reviewing, but why does it also have to include weekends and vacation? This is my time! Keep in mind the teacher alone is responsible for the direction and agenda of the classroom. Unless you are team teaching in which you may be fortunate to team with several hard working teachers. Otherwise, take an anger management class to cope with teachers who rarely prepare and expect you to carry the load.

There are professional curriculum advisors and guides, but only you can implement them. Nothing comes easy until you have repeated the lessons four or five times and made adjustments to correct glitches and identify methods to emphasize your goals. There is a need to be alert and take the time to locate materials related to my curriculum. It is hard to imagine all the places material can be located. Many magazines have pictures and articles which I need to analyze for the sections appropriate for students. Teacher specialty stores have many displays and visual materials related to my subject areas. One of the best sources is companies specializing in teaching materials since they have catalogs and materials designed by teachers. I will have to get a larger mail box and the mail carrier will need a weight training program to handle all the mail once my name gets on publisher lists. A diligent and conscientious teacher will modify the lessons to suit their philosophy and goals. Field trips by my class to locations which often have free or inexpensive brochures and postures provide materials for future display. I like to take vacation trips to locations that enhance knowledge and provide statues, books and media to present to students. If a person knows the right people, and doesn't mind losing your envious teacher friends, some trips can be taken during the school year.

The Real Deal

Old habits are hard to break and my addiction to journal entries isn't going away any time soon. So here I go again bearing my soul to the world. I wonder if anyone will take the time to read this? My Dad might say, "Damn the torpedoes, full speed ahead." When my students arrive,-notice this was a possessive pronoun, which means I have committed to another person because I now have a personal responsibility for their success. It's a feeling of caring about someone, and I will extend the extra effort to be sure they have the attitude and skills needed to pass the class. My advice is to swallow your pride, because this holds true even for those students who caused problems. There was a sign in the front of another teacher's room, "Students don't care how much you know, but want to know how much you care." We all remember hearing "first impressions are final", which means I need to provide a friendly but firm attitude the first few days. It reminds me of working for a crabby boss? Just a short interaction with a negative boss is depressing enough to make avoidance a primary goal at work. A student isn't likely to accept or remember what a grouchy teacher provides. It is difficult not to have a positive attitude around a leader who smiles frequently or at least has an approachable personality.

To create a positive attitude in myself and others I try to start positive. Whenever possible, I plan to stand near the door as students enter the room and just provide a positive "good morning" or hello to create a positive atmosphere. It is always supportive to mention and recognize personal student achievements in music, athletics, newspaper, plays, jobs or any activity which requires effort and commitment. To really make an impression mention the student achievement in front of the class, but you have to be careful not to overlook anyone. This can also become meaningless if done too frequently. Speaking of ambitious athletes, a young man hurrying home so he could return to wrestling practice stopped suddenly in the heavy dismissal traffic, and he was rear-ended by the school police officer. If this is not embarrassment enough, the next day the Officer who was always present in the lunch room, when suddenly he saw the young wrestler being carried on a stretcher by four of his buddies. The buddies were shouting "he did it", "he did it" in front of 800 students as they pointed at the Officer. Fortunately, the Officer had his Irish sense of humor and was friends with the young man.

Another Officer, in civilian clothes after dismissal, was riding his bike along a road used by many students traveling to and from school. Anything for a good laugh was the mantra as a group of rowdies hurled a piece of pipe from the car door into the spokes of his bike. The students then turned around and drove back to revel in laughter at the guy sprawled in the ditch. This promptly resulted in their arrest since he had no problem identifying the well known pranksters. A good lesson is to always know your target and the consequences.

The end of the school day is a lot like the last tune at a rock concert. Unbridled energy exploding in congested hallways. Teachers had an unwritten rule not to leave until fifteen minutes after student dismissal. Believe it or not this was not a rule enforced by the administration. This was a self imposed restriction in an attempt to live a few years longer. The parking lot was a dangerous place with youthful drivers' minds on escaping and having fun. Chaos is the rule, so that is why I decided to park on the safety of a side street. This is where I found my trunk caved in. Utilizing my Sherlock Holmes abilities I knew the vehicle had to be a raised frame to go over the bumper since my tail light was smashed. The next few days I searched the area and found a raised pickup with red plastic imbedded in the soft rubber of the bumper. The school police officer did the rest to get the damage repaired.

In the first day or two of the year it is important to present the goals of the class. How will this class help the student in seeking employment or to become successful in life? How will this course help me improve myself and become a better family member? Why is the class required? How will it help me in future classes and activities? Does the teacher have a regular cycle or schedule for tests, assignments and important presentations? How can I get make up work and how long do I have to complete it? These are just some of the questions that need to be answered the first few days to demonstrate you have solid goals and requirements.

Catering to students by changing your standards in reaction to a few complaints-destroys confidence of both students and the teacher. It's not just stubbornness and refusal to change, but failure to meet goals, and abandoning experience as to what students need to accomplish. I need to know myself and what I feel comfortable presenting. Since the ability to read the non-verbal is genetically programmed it allows students to perceive my confidence level. This is the area in which an experienced teacher has tested results, and knows exactly what and how to provide for the intended instruction. I don't make excuses or apologize for providing skills which are necessary for survival. Explain the goals and move on with confidence. I believe it was Lincoln who said it is better to remain quiet and thought a fool, than to open your mouth and remove all doubt. Every year I have gained confidence, and I know which words and phrases can be a distraction for students. Retaining focus on my lessons and goals will help students model my interest.

Respect for Whom?

With love I write to my journal, as I continue down a path which seems to be created just for me. Is this the way Alice in Wonderland felt? Oh well, back to reality regardless of the cost. Grades are of primary importance and students need to know exact standards. They need to know grades are not based on whether you like them. My personal experience was it didn't matter whether the teacher liked me or not. Just jump into the assignment and hope for the best. Pray that you understand the directions, and pay attention to what is going on around the room. As a teacher I had to struggle and sweat blood-to satisfy my conscience as to fairness with special attention to avoiding discouragement to any struggling student. If you don't know the rules, how can you play the game? For example, what are percentages of the grade is based on tests, assignments and class participation? Students often have different study techniques depending on whether teacher tests are essay, objective, or observational. Observational means student presentations, role playing or group work. Some students actually enjoy extra credit, and they need to know how it is factored into the grade. How much extra credit should I allow? Should I have designated projects or can students make suggestions?

Is there a need classroom rules? This depends on the age of the students and agreed upon rules by the faculty. Good luck with this one, as every faculty has several stubborn non-conformists who refuse to agree to common rules. One rule that covers many others is when students are reminded regularly to respect each other. This will create a cooperative and supportive classroom. Not only will students respect each other, but appreciate the fact that the teacher sees them as mature and capable of doing the right thing. Unless a teacher can cope with frequent disruptions, there may have to be a penalty for late arrival to class. One student came late half way through the class with the excuse of getting a drink of water. I asked if he choked at the fountain and needed CPR? Sometimes humor defuses the irritation.

I try to avoid looking like the near-sighted person who can't find their glasses or a totally disorganized bungler. Prior to the first day and again every day when there is a need for equipment I make sure to have access or bring it to my room. Students have become noisy without supervision due to the fact I had to look for an overhead projector. Who said anything about being disorganized? My mantra is to take extra time so I don't damage anything! The lesson may also call for a television so have the DVD or program set before the start of class so all I have to do is turn it on. Test the equipment before using it since locating someone to assist during class time is frustrating and sometimes impossible. I can recall several times when a tech minded student came to the rescue. We couldn't get the word captions off the picture. Maybe there was some benefit as some research says reading the captions without sound improves reading skills. Failure to check out equipment ahead of time might result in physical therapy which I needed to rehabilitate my finger. Holding a finger on a broken piece of the projector for 45 minutes was beyond my finger's strength and design. Pay attention to everything, since prior to DVDs my Dad tells of a 16mm film breaking in a darkened room. How do you keep 30 students calm for the time it takes to rewind a three foot pile of film?

Why should a teacher arrive in class before the students when ever possible? There was a time when I came a little late from lunch and a surprise was in store. I pulled down the overhead screen to begin a presentation only to see some student had taped a picture of a half-naked woman on it. Just look the class over and the faces will tell you who probably did the deed as they will be the first to laugh since they knew it was coming. However, knowing who probably did something wrong is never enough to make an accusation. A person doesn't want to stick their neck out and have it chopped off due to the lack of first hand observation. Nothing destroys a reputation and credibility faster than being unable to support an accusation with evidence. A teacher needs to be able to demonstrate fairness and facts to students, parents and the principal, therefore unsupported ranting will not help. On another occasion, I was about to point to a key location on a pull down map. After my demonstration, releasing the spring driven map rather quickly, it hit the bracket so hard and flew off. The map went over my head landing in front of me on the floor as I walked toward my class. The only thing more embarrassing would be if it had hit me in the head.

The teacher across the hall was walking through the gym as a shortcut to class in front of 300 students seated for a picture. A chant kept getting louder and louder with roars of laughter. "I'm blinded, I'm blinded" while covering their eyes. He was prematurely bald. Keep in mind we all have strong social motives to preserve our self esteem and reputation among our peers whether you are a student or teacher. It's always tempting to belittle or chastise a student in front of the class or a group since it will have a dramatic effect. Unfortunately, the embarrassment and loss of status for the student may create a person who has a strong desire to reestablish their previous peer acceptance. Now this is a situation where the degraded student will try to reestablish the peer status, but in ways that are not directly confrontational to the teacher. The instructor might experience unfounded rumors about competency or personal life. Several students could join their fallen comrade to embarrass the teacher by being uncooperative. So I have created a monster by the failure to provide respect to a person who may have previously respected me as a teacher. Next time, if fortunate enough to have one, I plan to either ask the student to stay after class or if it requires immediate attention to step out in the hall. Now we can talk in a calm but firm manner directly addressing the problem. This will make me appear more professional and adult like, but it is important to focus on the specific behavior. The conversation often deteriorates if another student's behavior enters the conversation. I explain to the student that the other student's problem will be my focus at a later time, but the student needs to accept responsibility for his or her own behavior. Usually, most students will agree to improve their attitude and behavior rather than escalating to the level of parental or principal involvement.

Treating a young person in an adult like manner will most often bring out their maturity. Also, an eye to eye conversation with an adult in a one to one situation is sobering, and not something most students want to experience. If the student is argument prone I may have to assign time after school to discuss the matter since leaving the class unsupervised for more than two or three minutes is not legally acceptable. The days of short tempered reactions and making your own rules are no longer an option in these days of run-away lawsuits.

In by gone days my Father explained students didn't just sit after school in detention. Since the overburdened custodian could not always clean the room the student dusted erasers, swept the floors and emptied waste baskets. He drove a school bus and there was a much worse penalty if you misbehaved on the bus. The student had to clean the bus floors which were so dirty not even Oscar of Sesame Street would enjoy the mess. Plus you had to ride the bus for an hour until the end of the route. He never mentioned spanking a student, but I heard of a Physical Education teacher with a paddle that had holes in it to dissipate the force, and it left small welts on your butt.

Organized Chaos

This message is to the best listener I have every known, right here in front of me absorbing ink from my pen. If I could just inject enough life into my journal so it could give feedback! Questions I need to ask myself! Do you need extra chairs for guests or student discussions in the front of the room? Have you located what you plan to present on the maps? Do you need a computer and a projection devise? Do you have your notes organized, and enough handouts for each student? How about clean transparencies and pens for the overhead? Being prepared for everything is beyond my comprehension. However, in an unprepared situation maintaining my poise is the only dignity I have left. I was ready to dismiss the class from an isolated corner classroom of an older building. Walking to the door to open it, and then stand there for an orderly dismissal. As I twisted with force the doorknob came off in my hand. At first, I stood there amazed and stupid looking at the doorknob in my hand. After a lot of shaking, the door would not open. Sitting on the floor yelling out the grated door vent at students and teachers passing down the hall was not only embarrassing but futile. If you have ever been in the halls with passing students you know how deafening the noise can be. "Over here, look down, over here!" After the hall noise subsided, the teacher next door came out of his room and heard my yell. He inserted the door stem to set us free.

My best friends are the people in the media center since they can help locate equipment and be sure it is reserved. Also, if printing is submitted early enough, the duplicated copies needed will be on time and properly formatted. Just be sure the student helpers can be trusted, or classes will have copies of tests before the teacher. When problems operating equipment arise, the media personnel are the first resort for help, and sometimes will even come to the classroom so the class is not disrupted.

I spent my first year in a school of 1200 which means not recognizing many students even after an entire year. Occasionally, a student from another school would wander into the halls looking for a friend, seeking a confrontation with a rival or just enjoying a stroll, and of course they had no accountability. My duty was to question the wandering students. If there was no valid destination, either walk them back to class or to the disciplinarian's office. This didn't please the teacher who probably had a better class when the trouble-makers were gone. If this wasn't enough to strain teacher friendships, turning habitual violators into the principal also created retaliations. We had a rule that hats were not worn in the building, of which most outside intruders were unaware. Talk about creating an obvious target for questioning! One trespasser went directly to a classroom to punch a rival and paid the price of losing a starting position on the basketball team. Another, trench coat wearing and hat pulled down, regular visitor was selling drugs at his favorite isolated hallway. Once again, he had no hall pass or ID tag and wearing sunglasses were all red flags. –What was he thinking that we were born yesterday? A school in a high foot traffic area near commercial areas is especially vulnerable to unwelcome drifters. Talk about the ultimate criminal insult by uninvited visitors. A teacher friend was looking out his large Art Room window on the third floor admiring his newly purchased motorcycle. He was about to show his pride and joy to a couple of students when a pickup truck pulled up next to the new Kawasaki. Two thieves lifted it into the pickup and drove away never to be heard from again.

The primary idea is to remain calm and in control of myself no matter how difficult a situation may be. If a person can not remain composed, then I have allowed myself to be controlled by others. My leadership has been lost unless I can reassert calmness and think clearly. Sometimes a person can remain too calm. For instance, the time the emergency alarm went off just after a new procedure had been added. We were now required to stay in the classroom during an intrusion threat or tornado warning. So in my calmness mode I instructed students just to stay in their seats and continue to work. They were enjoying the class activity and everything was upbeat even though two students asked why we were not evacuating. Little did I realize, since those exiting did not have to pass my doorway, that everyone else had left the building. Fortunately, no one checked my room so I did not get fired for this grievous error. In spite of making mistakes I try to keep my poise, and remember to treat students with respect. I am modeling behavior and students will in turn act respectful most of the time. Keeping to remind myself, a teacher must be fair but firm. Becoming a buddy will work for the short term, but eventually I realized a teacher has to be a leader and assert oneself. A buddy is open to immature remarks from friends which is perfectly normal. Many teachers lacking leadership have interesting yet not so complementary nicknames like Clueless, Spastic, Airhead and Bozo. Students need confident leadership to follow instructions, not someone who can be continually challenged and disrespected like a buddy.

Have I ever experienced a situation where I lost my poise and calmness? The lunchroom is a special place where everyone is in a hurry since it is crowded and time is limited. The place is so noisy you can barely hear the person next to you speaking. Students are trying to squeeze by each other with trays in hand and often dropping food on each other. Sorry about the mustard on your shoulder! Controlled chaos is a good way to describe it. I needed to have a hearing test since there was a question as to whether I was losing my hearing or my mind. A person is unable to converse with anyone standing next to them. The only place with higher crushing noise was a band at an assembly. Your mind will recover, but the ringing never stops. Every teacher should be prepared to be assigned to a duty that involves supervision of the lunchroom, school yard, restroom or halls. Unfortunately, it is easier for a principal to assign the same teachers for years. If you have the right schedule or don't complain you are a prime candidate for a difficult extra duty. An event that is unforgettable, concerns a fellow teacher who stepped in between two girls engaged in a full fledged fist fight. As the two combatants reached and grabbed for each other the teacher started turning to avoid blows and separate them. As she turned the three of them became a whirling dervish moving across the lunchroom. How could you forget that image?

Then there was the food fight, which became a popular emulation after a local rerun of the movie Animal House. All of a sudden, a student jumped up from a table yelling "food fight" and almost everyone else joined in. Composure deteriorated as teachers tried unsuccessfully to halt the turmoil which enveloped the entire room. Some tried to protect their clothing from flying ketchup and greasy burgers, but one unfortunate teacher who almost always wore a suit became a target. He was a former college football player and had no fear. So what if the missal hit him right in the chest wasn't he a massive target? Good grief, how could anyone look authoritarian with hot dogs and beans creeping down his shirt and tie and onto his pants. When the student saw the teacher charging after him he set a new land speed record to the outside door. The chase ended only when the teacher realized he was no longer playing football. Since there were no cameras and several hundred students were involved the penalty was cancellation of a school dance. Talk about escalation to make the situation worse, students then engaged in a sit-down strike by refusing to attend classes. Good advice is not to challenge a situation over which you know there is no control. A few teachers have no control over several hundred students who are determined to make a statement. Write down names and memorize behaviors assuming you don't get hit in the face which makes it difficult to write.

I discovered a referral to the Principal was a measure to be taken with caution for several reasons. First, it takes time to write up the details and it must be specific. For example, the student distracts others is not something that actually allows the Principal to specifically address the problem. The student may deny or say I was just turning around in my seat or the other student poked me. To add credibility to the referral, provide the number of times, words of the conversation, teacher warnings and other corrective measures taken. Vague accusations indicate a lack of effort by the teacher to correct the problem, and allow the student to manipulate the discussion. Trusting an overworked and parent pressured principal to handle problems may often result in disappointment. A teacher will develop confidence and respect of students by showing initiative by calling parents and personally conferencing with problem students.

By telephoning the parents when possible, a teacher can start with some positive remarks about the student which shows an interest in the student's best outcome. Then I can give exact details of what is happening without the filter of the Principal, and in stable households the parents will be able to address the problem more effectively than anyone. Also, I have not given up my classroom authority or interpretation of events to the principal, which can leave a strong impression on the student. Who knows, you may be on a positive public relations outreach since you are showing a personal interest in the student's achievement and personal development. Just like students, parents want to know you care. If nothing else, you might just make a friend, but don't count on it.

Extra Duties and Survival

Any new experience needs to be shared by my confidant and supporter which is no one other than my journal. Who else will actually listen to me? Maybe I should expose my duties outside the classroom. A teacher needs to carefully check extra-duty assignments so I will show up every day on time. An injury or assault in the area where you are responsible for supervision can result in a lawsuit. What can I expect for duties? Most often I could be found monitoring hallways, school grounds, lunchrooms and later in the day various school activities. Then there was selling tickets at the door or supervise behavior at dances and athletic events. Perhaps the most demeaning is supervising restrooms since you can encounter just about anything. Restrooms are smelly due to usage by large numbers, and it is one of the few hiding places in a school. As I approached the doorway the smell of marijuana drifted into the hall, but the place was empty. Eventually, drug users make a mistake so you must be patient. Then there were the two young males scrambling for their clothes all over the floor. I didn't even want to ask what was going on since their embarrassment was punishment enough.

Talk about making mistakes, I had a situation that caused one mistake to hurt me and a later on helped. I was headed to the locker room shower after a workout and left my locker door open which resulted in someone stealing my keys. When I say someone, the locker room had at least seventy young athletes who had access to my keys. How could I ever locate not only keys to inside and outside school doors, but also my house, car and personal keys? The situation was almost without hope when walking to lunch I passed by my assigned restroom. Several youngsters were laughing raucously, and as I glanced to the left, students were unable to enter or leave the locked door. Who said mistakes are always costly? Since I knew one of the laughers, the school police officer was contacted and he investigated. I was able to recover my keys to say nothing of my peace of mind. Talk about good timing, and it was quite awhile before I complained about restroom duty.

Speaking of restrooms it has always bothered me to see a custodian cleaning a stool that was deliberately clogged and running all over the floor. Frequently, they had to clean lipstick, ink or even waste off the mirrors and walls. This reminds me of an incident when some girls were caught leaving lip prints on the restroom mirrors. The principal invited them to the restroom to watch the custodian clean the mirrors. The custodian confidently dipped a brush in the stool and wiped it over the mirror before wiping it off. Funny, how a picture is worth a thousand words. Fortunately, most custodians do not become bitter and angry about this demeaning treatment. It puzzles me to know a student punishes a custodian in retaliation over an incident with a teacher or principal. I suppose it's transference of anger since the student would not directly confront a school authority. In spite of this treatment, I knew at least two custodians who where the most loyal supporters of school activities and students. They could be seen loudly cheering for various teams and complimenting students in the halls. No doubt they were also non-threatening counselors who assisted many students with personal problems.

There have been a few custodians who were given special recognition at parties or assemblies, which demonstrates most students reflect the American ideal of fairness and recognition of others. A custodian, who was protecting the school at Halloween when he ran on a flat roof toward some noise. Running on a roof means knowing when to stop. Predictably, he tripped and fell one and a half stories to the ground. After an embarrassing period of recovery he was able to work another Halloween. Another custodian was too curious as he cleaned the science area, and he was especially drawn to a small caged alligator. Only a chicken would be afraid to tease the gator by sticking a finger in the cage! How do you explain this emergency hospital visit to your supervisor? Always show respect to custodians since they fix the lights, can get a ladder when needed and know how to clean up various spills.

The school yard supervision requires eyes in the back of your head to monitor all the interactions happening simultaneously. Serious attention has to be given to anyone throwing objects, bullying and leaving the area. Most students will cease fighting when the teacher approaches, but in the upper grades there is less fear of authority and the teacher is at risk. Again, I remind myself to stay under control and use voice commands before forcefully trying to separate them. After the fighting ceases remove the offenders to an isolated place or room and talk to them one at a time. If you stay in the school yard friends will yell and interject comments which aggravates the situation. Get as many details as possible, and then write a referral to a principal to sort out more details and administer consequences. Why is it important to pay attention to details? I can recall a small twelve year old, who was being pummeled by another group of boys almost once a week. My first reaction was the aggressors were bullying, but as I talked with all involved I found an underlying cause. The small youngster was desperately seeking attention, and on a regular basis pestering and antagonizing the older group of boys. He was able to fulfill a need for recognition by his peers in a negative fashion. We all have a basic need to belong and accepted which is engrained in our personalities. Why the need for details as to what the offender was wearing, saying and behavior. Well, I had caught a student smoking in the restroom. Almost immediately the bell rang and we hurried to class, and the name he gave was bogus. I did not know him and could not describe his clothing. Even when he was identified again the principal rejected taking the offender to a required court appearance. Even though she had a good idea that it was a valid accusation the evidence was weak and uncertain.

Personalities Emerge

My journal knows me better than anyone especially when it comes to connecting with other people. How many people have a book as their best friend? Well, at least I can hold it close and next to my heart. As each day goes by a teacher begins to assess and evaluate students both on ability and attitude. These two elements do not always go together. Often the class leader and highly intelligent student is in desperate need of attention. This is a deadly combination since this student knows how to play the game by instigating others to say and do what he or she knows will disrupt the class. Somehow, this behavior pattern is genetically instilled and emerges as if needed for survival of the species. Just accept the fact that human survival demands this, and then you can engage and counteract with calmness and recognition. In other words, this person wants attention so interact in a manner that you have control by confirming some ideas presented and challenging others. We both win as students are often stimulated by the discussion and my interaction confirms my position of class control.

When I'm not engaged in correcting a student, and want to encourage discussion. I pause during remarks, as though I were thinking. This method allows students to include their ideas and develop a personal attachment to the topic or lesson. Often, they need just enough time to organize their thoughts and confidence. Most importantly, I need to direct my attention to the participating and respectful students. The number may vary, but these students are in every class. They need to be drawn out and reinforced for their behavior and importance to the class. This will not only improve the environment to one of mutual respect, but provide support and encouragement to the teacher.

When problems arise, which will occur in every class, I mentally focus on the positive behavior experienced with the respectful students. This frame of mind is essential to maintain a calm and respectful overall attitude toward all students regardless of their past behavior. Students can be brutality honest which is a good quality for sincere friendship. Sometimes they overlook how humiliating the truth can be. I was standing in front of the class when a young man, who tried to be respectful, presented me with a bottle of mouthwash. He spoke clearly and loudly that I really needed this gift. Not only will I not forget to use mouth wash, but started carrying breath mints. Not only that, countless hours were spent researching facial expressions and non-verbal behavior when I came near someone.

Believe it or not, I have gone home with a good feeling and attitude. My home life will actually be relaxed and confident rather than worrisome and stressed over the problems of the day. Just by creating my primary focus on the respectful students, enables me to enjoy the classroom activity and interact positively with everyone. Tired after a long day, I was all ready to head home after talking with a student about a project. The student had just left and the three books I desperately needed to prepare to tomorrow's lessons were missing. The books were later discovered in his locker which he had accidentally picked up-from my desk. From then on paranoia developed when students placed their books on my desk. Another important attitude I need to develop is to say a positive hello to students when passing in the halls and at school events. This greeting is a way to express to students that they are important and worthwhile of recognition. We all enjoy having someone of stature confirm we are deserving of attention. Does the need for obsessive attention exist? A sobbing young lady came into my room lamenting her failure to be selected for a musical. Her emotions seemed to dominate her life as she crashed and burned frequently. She was married before graduation even though she was not pregnant.

Strange, how this getting attention behavior powerfully overwhelms a person. While seated at my desk, I kept hearing a loud clink on the blackboard to my left. Maybe it was someone was hitting the wall on the other side, but I decided to investigate. What are these coins doing on the floor? Do I have a hole in my pocket? Suddenly, it occurred to me that someone threw the coins through the open door. Running to the back of the room to see who was in the hall, but when no one was there I went back to my desk. Another loud clink and I ran to the door again, but no one was in the hall. As I walked back to my desk I saw some coins on the top of a desktop. This was the same guy who earlier in the year helped release some guinea pigs from another room. When I didn't notice-the pig, he loudly demanded to know why the animal was sitting behind me. And I thought it was just celebrities who needed attention. Speaking of attention, let's face it there is little or no privacy in a classroom. All those bodies jammed into a small area-nothing escapes attention. I had to have a large sack to carry a project to class, and this pink one I found at home was perfect size. As usual and in a hurry, who

cares what is written on the outside of the bag? Why did I have to leave it in front of the room where everyone could recognize it was from Victoria's Secret? How do you explain this to a hormone driven group of teens?

Attitude is Everything

I've had some good days and all I need to do is to read my journal to build my self esteem. Who ever heard of a teacher with low self esteem? Don't they always look confident in front of adoring students? Well, maybe in their dreams! Students appreciate someone who cares enough about them to make a sacrifice to attend school events or any other activity. I am really tired after standing on my feet for almost six hours or more, and exhausted from rushing from room to room and around the room facilitating students and materials. My feet feel like I just finished a marathon, and my head pounds like a sledgehammer. How can anyone expect me to correct papers after school, for which there will not be enough time to finish? Then, rush home to eat and return to school for an activity? Students also do this and understand the time and energy involved, and this is why it means so much. I can actually enjoy the play, dance or athletics if all goes well. Most of the time students are well behaved, but I am still on duty as a school employee. I might even have an opportunity to visit with a student or two in a situation which does not have the restriction of a classroom. You can be yourself which allows students to know you personally. Well, maybe knowing my personal life might not be such a good thing.

However, when a student throws an object at another fan or participant you have to take action by confrontation or reporting the incident to authorities. Even more demanding is the use of alcohol or drugs since this is often concealed, and most teachers probably don't carry alcohol or drug testing equipment. Always be careful where standing or sitting since occasionally a drink or mud ball can come hurdling down from behind creating apprehension as to who was the intended target. Not much doubt however, when your name is yelled. You might try to avoid sitting next to a parent, however, most will be delighted to meet you. Those with an axe to grind will require your skills as a defense attorney. If you are not their child's teacher, try defending a teacher even if you don't like them. Even though I can not completely relax and enjoy the event, most of the time there are no incidents. Teaching in a school which has well publicized disciplinary policies, and is willing to enforce them helps the word go out and minimizes problems. The risk of misbehavior is worth the pay off which means connecting to students in more ways than just as a teacher. I now feel like a friend or parent who has a personal interest rather than just a job to do or professional duty.

How far will you go to help students participate in activities? It was a late spring and the snow was piled two feet deep on the running track across from our building. Fortunately, only half the track was covered with snow, but it still took me two days after school to remove enough snow so we would have at least two lanes for running. Another late spring storm found me standing in the entry of the school bus with the door open so the driver could be told where the edge of the road was located. He would have to have Superman's X-Ray vision to see through a 40mph snow storm. It was amazing we actually made it back 15 miles while only seeing the edge of the road. We returned to the indoor track facility where I had the unforgettable experience of sleeping on a weight bench. My legs were stiff for a week, and how could I ever have expected to sleep with at least 300 screaming athletes playing basketball and tag all night? Most teachers are familiar with school activities and know what they are dealing with. To avoid embarrassment always check out proper rituals and behavior of cultural and religious events. A teacher friend of mine was invited to a young student's Bar Mitzvah at the synagogue. As he entered the well attended gathering he donned a scull cap as required by males. Eyes were on this red headed guest as he proceeded to the front and prominently genuflected before entering his seat. It's almost as bad as referring to the incorrect culture when attending a graduation reception or cultural fair.

After the long day, which sometimes has begun with an extracurricular activity at 6AM, classes are the next priority. Even though in this situation there is no preparation time before classes begin, the need for an interesting lesson is still paramount. Why start so early? The gym is used all day long and the only time available is early in the morning, and you are grateful for the opportunity. So how can I deal with these time constrains? The answer lies in even more preparation. Life is easier and less stressful by developing lesson plans at least one week and possibly two weeks before classes. This is risky since teachers are often not informed as to changed class schedules more than one or two days in advance. Nevertheless, it is easier to shorten and switch class activities on my plans rather than develop new plans late at night or minutes before classes begin. What happens to those who are not prepared? It's like not finding your car keys when you are already late for work. Nothing diminishes a teacher's leadership more than uncertainty in the classroom. These fatal flaws are easy to read by students, and as soon as the teacher feels confused all bets are off. Students begin to look at each other to groan or laugh not necessarily to ridicule, but because they have experienced this lost feeling many times. How fast can you lose face? Try standing in front of the class with a puzzled look because you can't figure out why they are smiling and grinning. Just look down and notice your shirt pocket is all red from an ink pen. I might be able to survive two or three well spaced loss of direction and focus incidents. Any more teacher confusion often will cause students to stereotype me into a disorganized buffoon.

How can I avoid looking like an incompetent degree holding loser? The answer can be summed up in three words: prepare, prepare and then prepare again. Lesson plans have various standards of preparation depending on the administration's requirements. If there is no set style then I like to create a format which will be easy to read at a glance. It is almost impossible to condense information into the small blocks provided by the school lesson plan booklet so abbreviate and use two or three colors of ink. The neatness and completeness depend on whether the administration collects lesson plans either weekly, at the end of the term or not at all. I like to write in the media presentations first since use of equipment often requires a reservation. I always remind myself to enter any early dismissals or presentations students are required to attend before developing a plan for the day. We absence minded humans like to make last minute changes almost as much as losing car keys. When there is an unannounced program I try to avoid rewriting the lesson by using a bright colored pen to cross-out or modify, or if possible, use arrows to move the lessons around.

For many years I rummaged through written lessons stored in my desk looking for what could be used each week. At least there was no need to rewrite each lesson, but it was still time consuming. Eventually, I came to conclusion that organized folders would work just fine. A person can duplicate the lessons plans intended for reuse. Giving close attention as-to how the activity could be modified to-provide the best method of student instruction. Also, I ask myself if the lesson was adaptable to other presentations. Should the material be presented in group work, individual research, role play, lecture or an alternate technique? There are textbooks that should go through a book burning. Read them carefully I, there has to be something useable inside those covers. Try to coordinate the lessons with the chapters of the textbook containing similar material. On the other side of the question, I found the textbook often has more information than could possibly be provided during class. One of the most important messages to instill in students is their obligation to set high standards of achievement by reading and studying outside of class. Unfortunately, our educational system has placed so much emphasis on teacher competence that student responsibility has been overlooked. Many students have the impression that if they show up and listen in class they will have all the knowledge necessary for success. Why can't I absorb knowledge through my skin while I sleep? What a cruel hoax and deception. We forget almost ninety percent of what we see and hear within 24 hours unless it is frequently reinforced. Students need to talk to each other about understanding the material, and read a more in-depth explanation to successfully retain the knowledge. What do you mean my boyfriend/girlfriend doesn't want to talk about class material? Don't they want a better grade or even a job?

Returning to the lesson plans, I now need to look at my folders or material selected for presentation and determine the amount of time to allocate. Careful monitoring the activity during class, and writing down the time needed certainly helps this determination. Time allocation is a crucial part of the lesson since not completing the activity destroys the objective by not allowing a conclusion and evaluation. A delay until the following day for follow up reinforcement removes the full effect of what was to be accomplished. My confused mind requires me to make notes in the lesson as to which students will be the most effective leaders. If you are far enough into the school year to know the students this determines the success of a lesson. It's like the NFL draft when selecting a good team since your job depends on it. Sometimes you may need to talk to a student the day before so they can come prepared to play a role. Just hope and pray they show up for class unless you have alternate plans. The success of the activity will often depend on which students are selected as leaders. Some are born to lead and love the attention. Others are only interested in getting a laugh from their peers and making the teacher look ridiculous. Looking ridiculous is often not difficult! Some lessons will have to wait until you know your students so you can make first selections of leaders with success. After awhile almost any student can volunteer and be chosen since hopefully the teacher has established credibility and good judgment. If you show hesitancy or uncertainty student confidence diminishes, and future risk taking by volunteers will be lacking. What additional materials are needed to have ready and in what numbers? Is there equipment needed? What can I say or do if a student is reluctant or embarrassed to participate?

One teacher had a grading system he called stair step evaluation. He jokingly told students he stood at the top of the stairs and threw the papers down. The A's landed at the top and F's at the bottom of the stairs. For motivational purposes, an evaluation method should be explained to students prior to the activity since this improves lesson quality. Students could write a paragraph explaining what they learned, or complete a ranking scale to indicate what they retained. There could also be a short verbal or written quiz, or I could record names to award participation points as part of the overall grade. The teacher needs to continually monitor student reaction to the lesson, and whether they are actually learning the material presented.

A good lesson plan should always have ready a 15 to 20 minute extra credit or additional assignment related to the intended lesson. What is the purpose of this supplement? Sometimes the student discussion of the primary lesson will be brief if it is beyond the interest or comprehension of the class. The written work could be less difficult than was anticipated so students finish early. Therefore, students who finish early should have the option of answering a worksheet or essay questions for extra grade points. This will help avoid their distraction of students still working on the primary assignment. I provide scaled credit for the amount finished to compensate for those who vary in the amount of time available after they finish the required assignment. To provide teacher credibility and student incentive, place the extra points at the top of the returned paper and incorporate into the grade. All extra credit work should have an educational purpose which can be difficult for some teachers to grasp. Teachers have been known to give extra credit for having their car washed, delivering messages, cleaning the room, and correcting papers. Can you believe it?

It isn't just the content of the lesson; put how it is presented that makes the difference. If the teacher is enthusiastic and confident many students will absorb these feelings. Americans in general respond to excitement and leaders with enthusiasm. Just look at popular entertainers, politicians and leaders who capture massive attention because they have strong feelings for their agenda.

Guest speakers are an exciting and credible manner in which to present important objectives of a lesson. A Geography class addressed by a person living in Nigeria, France or Turkey, who may be close to the student ages, can have a long lasting impression. Also, I award extra credit to students who make contacts with acquaintances to invite guest speakers. Students can be successful with an invitation since the guest speaker is often a personal acquaintance. First hand experiences of judges, police officers, veterans, bankers and missionaries are just a few possibilities. I can remember having a recovered multiple personality present information about her illness. Everyone was wondering if she was actually in her core or real personality.

No matter how you try to control activities sooner or later something breaks down. For example, we were studying non-verbal expression to see if a person were lying. This lesson was intended to determine how closely a person pays attention to non-verbal communication, not just spoken words. Four students were selected, and then standing in front of the class doing their best to tell a personal story without revealing whether it was truthful or lies. Only one student was telling the truth. Prepare yourself, since there is no control over what the topic will involve. A young man, who apparently was not lying due to the details, explained how his father worked as a pimp in Chicago. Another young lady told a story of being slapped by her mother. And finally, if you are ever stopped by the police, and are about to be arrested consider this. When a person is about to lose their drivers license, and you feel mindlessly desperate, try sympathy. A girl's best defense is to cry uncontrollably. The class was told "It works every time."

Groups Need Structure

My journal is not private and it holds the key to my personality and my group of friendships. On second thought, maybe I should keep it private since my personality is rather confusing. If I can't figure it out, who can? All I know is my personality is the key to teaching. What should I be doing if the students are engaged in presentations, role playing or discussion groups? Hopefully, not dozing off in the back of the room! What should not be done is to sit on a chair at the back or front of the room no matter how tired a person is from late nightlife. There is a need to circulate among the groups to see if they are engaged in the assigned task or just socializing. Also, verify who is actually doing the work and deserves extra credit. I feel like a mother hen, but the social forces are too great to avoid monitoring assigned written tasks by individuals or groups. Sometimes it is beneficial to sit with the group to provide hints or suggestions, but be careful. Just get them started and then leave with an understanding I will return shortly. In this way a teacher will not be conned into doing the work for the individual or group. Whether on the job or in school, dependence on others destroys confidence and initiative. Proximity of the teacher brings out good work habits in students. However, when an individual or group is making a presentation in front of the room, a teacher needs to be off to the side or at the rear paying attention as a model to the class. Talking or walking in front of students making a presentation is rude, and distracts them from the lesson. Why are we so desperately in need of attention?

It is important to Show courtesy and respect which allows the presenter to feel validated as to what they are saying. Some pointers I need to remember is not allowing students to switch from group to group during the class activity for two reasons. First, students need to work and interact with various individuals, not just their selected friends. This will help them in their future employment. Second, the peer pressure will often form groups with a social agenda, and the group will have a difficult time staying on task. Always be careful where you sit if you are moving around the room since some students love to change the focus and create chaos. I have pulled tacks out of my butt, and tried to remove gum and bodily fluids from my backside. No doubt the torturous items were intended for a student. Don't you agree? Everybody loves me.

What are some possibilities for group activities? Almost any assignment can be adapted to groups if I follow some guidelines. Provide handouts with a list of questions to be answered or essay questions for a reaction to reading material. Each time explain how the grade will be established, and it helps to recognize leadership and effort with individual grades. Determine a point scale for the person who verbally speaks to the class, extra points for writing the summary for the group, and credit for focus and enthusiasm. Sometimes more grade weight will be given to participation if the group is engaged in role playing or demonstrations. Since I usually will be busy observing and listening there will probably be a delay until the next day to provide the grades. Not good, but it can't be avoided. Sometimes group activities can be risky and even flooring. There was an engaging class group activity related to trusting others which involved forming a circle of trust. A person in the middle must close their eyes and fall backward to be caught, and then pushed upright to fall in the opposite direction. Arms must be at your side, eyes closed, and feet together so you are completely vulnerable to the group. After several students had shown their trust, we were looking for one more person to volunteer. I volunteered when no one else stepped forward. Talk about lack of supervision and organization when the teacher is no longer in charge. Stepping into the center thinking all were ready, I then awakened with a pain in my derriere and head after hitting the floor. This certainly demonstrated trust, but my learning experience was to keep my eyes open until everyone is ready. Who said you can't trust people?

My first rookie group experience was a disaster. I can recall when I first attempted to organize students into small groups for discussion as I had observed another teacher successfully utilize. Live and learn from your mistakes as the group work deteriorated into a noisy, unorganized chaos as students were out of their groups and pestering friends. What I had failed to comprehend was the need for goals and accountability. Don't we all need this? Each group needed a guide or list of questions to be answered and shared with the class.

A time frame was needed to keep them on task with frequent reminders as to the amount of time remaining. Also, a group base grade to which additional points would be awarded to the writer, speaker and any demonstrated leadership. There was a need to remember that unless there is group accountability the process deteriorates into socializing. I almost overlooked the fact that in this

first attempt at group work, one adventurous student seated near the door left the room without permission. He must have taken advantage of me when I turned my back to help someone. The wandering student was later discovered hiding in a clothes dryer used by the athletic department. I guess he was trying to come clean.

New Teachers

This is a good day and it's so obvious, I tell my journal, that I made some new friends with people who need me. Yes, there are people who need me in spite of my faults. I also need them as is obvious in the following situations. A new teacher's best resource is their fellow teachers. Here is a case in point of someone I admired and disliked at the same time. I watched in awe as he walked into the room and students brought themselves under control to listen. There were no demands for attention and no threats to pay attention. He then sat on the edge of the desk and began talking in a soft voice with no student interruptions, and no need to seek out and demand attention from students who were more interested in their friends. How does this happen? Does he have a magical spell? I did read about a frustrated teacher, as a last resort effort, began sprinkling the class with some voodoo preparation to cast a spell of calmness. There was no need for potions in the case of this teacher who was admired by all. As I drew information from other teachers I discovered he was always calm, and held two positions which were coveted by students. He had the unusual combination of Band or Music instructor and basketball coach. It was revealed that his calm expectation for attention had been cultivated over many years, and students respected this approach in an adult. He apparently respected the students and encouraged their achievement. We all can't be coaches and music instructors, but we can all develop an environment of respect and self control. Yelling will command attention, but it is only temporary and frequently has to be reinforced with more yelling. Not only that, it is exhausting and stressful. It will shorten a career, and probably your stress filled life as well. It's like digging your own grave.

What else needs to be modeled in teachers who are successful? What I see is they seem to be well organized and work long hours which apparently is combination that can not be separated. For students to have a genuine interest in the subject feedback on achievement needs to be the day following the lesson. In order to accomplish this, depending on the student's age, the outside of class assignment needs to be around thirty minutes-due to the multiple effect of work from other teachers. Always be certain the assignment has a direct relationship to the material to be learned, and is not just busy work. Therefore, it can be completed in the next day or two, corrected immediately, and results returned the next day. Tests should be given regularly and results provided within one or two days. All of this keeps students engaged and interested, otherwise the learning curve of diminishing memory will create a lack of motivation. So a well organized and hard working teacher will instill in students the importance of extra effort. At the very least, this is a good way to motivate my own efforts.

My model teacher should have traits that promote the impression of being firm, fair and friendly. One or two of the traits will not provide the correct message. All three are necessary. For example, a firm person has definite goals of achievement both academically and socially. The firmness is respected by students because it shows a strong commitment to the importance of the subject and the need of the student to master the material. Also, students will try to convince you to ease up, but like a coach's demands they will respond with effort to demands for work. In regard to fairness, we are looking at the basic equality issues of our Constitution. Most students reject elitism and will not respect anyone who does not provide equal opportunity for everyone. Special treatment of a few, unless a disabled person, allows the student to establish a basic right to reject the teacher with the support of others. Can a teacher be too friendly? A pleasant and accepting attitude can be difficult when conflicts and problems occur, but respect grows as students admire a person who can handle a volatile situation. At the extreme; I knew a teacher who yelled insulting names and received insults in return. Could anyone determine who was actually the young person? Age is certainly not the measure of maturity. It was embarrassing and disturbing to watch.

On the opposite side of the scale is the stand-in for Genghis Kahn. If you have ever worked for a boss who is crabby imagine a student who can't quit the job, and has to face this grouch everyday. I was observing as a student teacher a veteran teacher who had a put-down for almost every student in the room. She was either intimidated and wanted to control the students, or came from a family where insults were acceptable. Somehow, insults tend to describe the person expressing them. Also, the moderately friendly person is using respect for others as a guideline, and provides a message to students that they are worthwhile even though they may have caused a serious problem in the past. You can not be a buddy, since students need leadership and guidance not someone who is needy of acceptance and vacillating when trying to please everyone.

Are Grades Necessary?

Dear journal, I am giving my best effort to tell this story right even though the details are complicated. Human interactions are often beyond easy understanding. My basic instincts usually get me through personality conflicts. People are pretty much the same wherever I find them. There will always be a few students who have little or no concern about the grade they receive. This could be a low expectation cover up so they won't feel bad when the actual grade is less than they could have achieved. However, due to our competitive society, employment goals, college acceptance and parental expectations most students work hard to achieve a passing grade. The key is the parental support and expectation since well motivated students will do well in spite of poor teaching methods. Most of the time, if the parents want high achievement the student will find a way to fulfill this goal. The difference between an A, B or C can be crucial for the high achiever. I am sure each teacher feels their method of calculation and percentages is the best, and the large variations will drive a statistician over the brink. My objective tests and exact measurements had me feeling confident. However, subjective evaluation creeps into the type of test questions selected, use of essay questions and evaluation of participation. Will Durant said, "Education is a progressive discovery of our ignorance."

The teaching style will play a large part in the grading scale and philosophy. I enjoy class activities since they require student involvement, emotional expenditure and physically demonstrate the purpose of the lesson. I crashed to the floor onto my butt and split my pants in an effort to be involved. Therefore, my system allows considerable weight to volunteering and participation in the class activities. A person could make 30 to 40 percent of the grade based on participation. Participation could also include answering questions during discussions as well as class activities, and should also reflect attendance to class. The remaining 60 to 70 percent of the grade is based on tests and assignments, but there are caveats in this area. Obviously, a test should confine questions to what was presented in class activities, discussion, lecture and text book material. Since teacher test questions are selected from content, and lack standardized test validity grading should be curved to adjust for many variables and shortcomings. In most subject areas everything can not be presented in class so reading the text book is crucial. This approach is important for college preparation since reading and studying on-your-own at a higher level will be expected. Standardized tests are excellent to determine acquisition of academic skills, but not what was presented in a learning unit with specific outcome skills and knowledge. A single test is limited when covering material presented over four or five weeks, so a standardized test utilized once a year is certainly deficient in scope and measurement.

Should extra credit be allowed? Some teachers feel students do not study the required material and rely on extra credit to pass the course. Again, my philosophy determines whether extra credit will be allowed. In our society we tend to reward hard work and extra effort so it would seem this idea should apply to the classroom. Perhaps, there should be a compromise on this issue by placing a limit on the amount of extra credit. For example, a student could be allowed only four extra projects or assignments each nine weeks or semester. I tend to grade the extra credit according to quality, but equally important is the amount of effort. There was a seventh grade student who had created a plaster of Paris mold of the United States and spent hours painting and labeling it. He carried it in his extended forearms through the doorway, and since it was an older building there was a raised threshold. I had personally tripped over this hidden structure about every other day. When his foot hit the stubbed nosed object, the plaster of Paris map flew up and crashed to the floor into fifty pieces. What can you do? I have had many hopeless situations, but there is no way to reconstruct this art work. Fortunately, it happened in front of me and not outside or at home so I could justify my evaluation. The pieces were lying on the floor, but the effort and detail was obvious. With this in mind, a decent grade was awarded. Haven't we all wanted to be rewarded for extra effort?

Sooner or Later

I have confidence that solving problems and understanding people is much easier once I explain them to my journal. Maybe it is because I can mentally move outside and reflect on the situation. Sooner or later there must be accountability for what has been happening in the classroom. Sure, there is a lot of independence to determine how the subject matter is provided to students and the amount of effort that is expended to attain achievement goals. Everyone is accountable to someone and I am no exception. The first person to consider is the principal, and like any employment a good relationship with the boss is the key to success. How to sabotage a friendship and create a hostile environment? Well, this teacher I know was successful in winning basketball games, but little did he know the opposing coach would be his future principal. The competition was intense and the payback for several defeats was cruel. Finding myself standing near and repeatedly checking a smelly restroom or assigned to an ear-ringing noisy lunchroom with 800 students can be the "reward" for irritating the boss.

How many times and ways does a person have to be evaluated? Most principals just want someone who is dedicated to student achievement and who has good personal relationships. Principals are very professional and interested in supporting teachers since their success depends on the quality of work by their teachers. Principals have a lot of high stress and conflicting positions since they must accomplish a satisfactory affiliation with parents, teachers and the school board. These three groups are often at odds as to goals and methods of achievement. Talk about an impossible conflict of interests. How do they sleep at night?

Parents have a wide variety of educational expectations depending on whether they emphasize social acceptance, educational achievement or both. I can recall parents who wanted exact details on lessons and behavior as compared to those who were very blasé about everything. Most of the time parents want the truth as to what a child is accomplishing. The most important question is what the parent and student can do to improve. A few parents feel somewhat helpless because the child has taken control and has become defiant or apathetic about achievement. Often there is a brief improvement after conferences, and then a slide back into old habits of lacking ambition. One of the best ideas I have seen is the parent bringing the student to conferences. Students frequently have doubts about what was said to their parents because some teachers present only a favorable evaluation and others emphasize the negative. Why did you tell my parents I was sleeping in class? Good question, should I take a picture next time? A picture cell phone could send the incident to Mom or Dad immediately. When the student is present honesty should be honored since the student can challenge remarks either at the conference or later. Most students are rather sheepish when confronted with poor attendance or low grades because Mom and Dad are looking at them for an answer. Parents who are hearing about problems and are in a hurry to get it over with often do not follow up with suggestions for student improvement. Parents who ask for a follow up phone call or letter want student accountability and improvement.

Perhaps the sadist situation is the parent who rarely or never shows at conferences. What is the message to the student? School is not important, and I really do not care what you are doing. How can anyone be successful without some positive reinforcement? There were several confrontational situations with parents that could easily have deteriorated into a yelling match. The key is to remember I am a professional, and there is a need to remain calm, confident and factual. When a parent is hostile from the start either the student has lied to them about events or they have a previous prejudice. As a coach, there were times I brought out some angry reactions from players and fans. Conferences can often take some strange twists and turns from unexpected events. One parent, who was later discovered to be a star player on an opposition team we had defeated, decided I lacked motivation to inspire her child to work. She and her friend were accusatory from the start and the best that could be done was to speak honestly and calmly. Another wife of a fellow teacher accused me of being an anarchist since it was defined and examined in class. We were studying Geography and political systems of various countries. There was no reference to acceptance of any radical philosophy. Maybe it was the camouflage shirt I was wearing.

So what if you might be tired after teaching all day and then conferencing for an additional 4 to 5 hours? Jim apparently lost self control and the conference deteriorated into a yelling match. Then, the testosterone engaged and the two had a fist fight. When children are involved emotions are high. Have you ever been witness to the hostility of parents at a youth league game? I like to shake hands and greet parents in a friendly manner which is something we all appreciate. Also, it is important to present the positive information first to indicate I am on the side of student achievement, and later work into the areas needing improvement. A person might have to fantasize to find something positive, but it will be worth it. I focus on the student and not the academic experiences of the parent who sometimes believes problems are genetic. My grade book is more important than this journal since I need facts not guesses about grades and attendance. It's not senility affecting your exhausted memory at this time of day. Sometimes parents will allow you to view the report card to see all the student grades from other teachers. This could be helpful to determine if he or she is doing poorly only in my class. There is a need to determine if the problem is student effort, lack of basic skills or personal problems. Occasionally, other students can be a problem in a class by distracting a friend or even worse intimidating a student. I have seen numerous occasions of students changing classes due to problems with other students. A symbiotic relationship between students tends to bring out the worst behaviors in both youngsters. This happens even when they don't particularly like each other.

Frequently, I expect to telephone a parent if there is a problem, and occasionally a there will be phone contact from a parent. Does human nature change our interactions on the telephone as compared to personal contact? Most of us have a tendency to be more direct and make comments on the phone that we would avoid saying in person.

When I can not see the non-verbal reaction or hurt look on a person's face there is a tendency to be more aggressive and honest. We are much braver and confrontational since the long distance insulates us from retaliation. If we have not personally met, there is a normal tendency to create a preconceived image or stereotype. This image is difficult to correct or readjust over the telephone since we need a lot more personal contact and interaction to overcome negative ideas. So I want to assume the best concept of the person on the other end of the line and attempt to maintain a positive conversation. Calmness and friendly attitude will achieve much more than immediate criticism of the student because this naturally initiates a defensive position by any parent. When friendly, try to be honest if there is reasonable expectation to correct the problem. Plan to emphasize the goal which is to help the child so he or she will succeed in school. There is a need to always have my grade book when calling since the topic will eventually involve the crucial question of the grade, assignments and attendance. I remind myself, don't call parents at work unless they request it since they may not have privacy or permission to discuss personal matters. Several calls seemed to be total failures since I had no idea who I was talking with due to language barriers. Was this a brother, sister, cousin or parent? In spite of the difficulty in communication, the next day the student involved often had a changed attitude and was working harder. The family apparently understood a lot more than I realized and made this known to the student.

If the problem involves other students, express the need for reassigning seating arrangement as much as possible. The students may be close friends who distract each other and keeping them apart is difficult. Can you imagine calling a friend before school to find out what to wear? Not eating lunch because someone else is seated next to your friend? I expect to get some complaints and resistance to seating changes, but being firm and decisive reinforces my leadership. Check the desk to be sure it is the right size, and don't create a worse problem by moving them near someone who is even more distractive. Some students do best in the front of the room and others in the back. Only trial and error can determine this. Size does make a difference in a seating arrangement, especially when the incredible hulk in front only allows a person side vision. I always consider physical size, hearing and vision factors. When successful, this allows everyone to learn and achieve. Disruption of the learning environment steals from all students' learning opportunities and this may never be recovered.

Satisfaction beats Happiness

This is a good day and I want to be sure my journal, who knows me best, has the reasons recorded. More than anything else I need to enjoy being involved with young people. At least most of the time! Consider their energy and zest for life. Since they don't have the scars of very many failures they tend to have an optimistic outlook of seeing the positive view of people and events. Watching the excitement when a young person meets a friend in the hallway or at social events is an inspiring event. They can hardly contain their excitement and are jumping, hugging or screaming with delight at just seeing a friend. One of the greatest challenges of teaching is adjusting and containing all of your emotions long enough to focus on the lesson. It is easy to get caught up in all the contagious activity, but experience has proven my calmness is needed to focus on the lesson and achieve the learning goals. Happiness is difficult to achieve and even harder to maintain, but satisfaction is a long lasting reward than can be shared and preserved with another person.

What is the one criterion that stands above all others as to whether a person will be successful as a teacher? More than anything else I believe the crucial element is helping young people succeed. Students often work extremely hard to create projects for contests, and the teacher shares in that success. Often the teacher receives awards and media attention. Coaches have a special relationship involving competition as teams sacrifice and struggle for a winning season. However, I admire the teacher who can identify positive characteristics in students who engage in severe behavior and attitude problems. It takes amazing patience and talent to work day after day for successful outcomes in a student who rarely shows any progress.

Keep in mind that a positive attitude is necessary since humans are so complex, and we all have various forces pushing in different directions. The problems at home may involve divorce, abuse or addictions, and the student needs to resolve these serious issues before moving on. I need to be ready for disappointments after spending hours talking and helping a student especially when they chose to drop out or fail. Often the teacher was successful even if the student failed the course since they discovered people do care about them. Students remember someone providing encouragement and direction, and they may pass this on to others.

Now that I know what I want to accomplish as a teacher how can all this be implemented? The reference is to motivation which is the key to all learning and accomplishments. So what is needed to initiate a motivational strategy? We all need heroes and I can visualize at least two or three teachers whom I admire. I can see them as satisfied with their everyday accomplishments and contact with students. In spite of criticism they receive for performance or handling of disciplinary matters they stay composed and positive toward others. These teachers can see good in everyone and even the worst confrontation has a good explanation and purpose. I can remember a teacher whose wife's sister was near death from cancer, and some students without knowledge of this decided to retaliate. They were irritated after being removed from an extra-curricular activity.

Let's punish the teacher by making repeated anonymous phone calls late at night causing anxiety and stress. If a person has ever received one of these shattering calls regarding the death of a loved one a person won't forget it. When the student's calls were traced, and they were apprehended the teacher had to decide whether to prosecute. He realized the potential of the students could be destroyed considering they had excellent ability and potential. The positive concern for others resulted in a school suspension rather than criminal charges. At a later date, two other teachers were physically assaulted by students, and yet they were able to forgive and forget the incident. So a motivating factor to become the best teacher possible will be to see the positive side of all encounters.

My motivation can also be enhanced by realizing students can provide positive reinforcement. How many times have I had a student remark that without my assistance they would not have been successful in school? Not only do students express appreciation, but many have positive and delightful personalities which infect those around them. I feel good just saying hello when some students enter the room. Their smile changes my attitude from suspicion to one of unconditional acceptance of others. It's like an energy drink! Now I can even make a fool of myself interacting with those who are quietly sullen or even grouchy with newly acquired enthusiasm.

My life as a teacher has often been charged with various emotions. How about students who had cancer and died? Fortunately there were only six, most of which occurred after they left my class. I can still visualize where they were seated, and their personal interactions that defined our relationship. The only consolation is awareness of the good they provided to others, and realize we are all on the same path. Others were confined to wheelchairs or abused by alcoholic parents, and yet were always able to smile and look forward to being with friends. How can I not love to go to work and be around young people who give me a positive attitude? Some are real characters who enjoy a brief entertaining song just before class or can tell a good joke or say hello in a dozen different ways. One young man I remember loved to put on a show. Often, he would mimic my behavior which fellow students loved to watch. His antics were always good natured and he knew when to quit. However, on a day when some important class evaluators were visiting, he came into the room to do a quick dance in front of the class. Since he was no longer in my class he then retreated to another classroom. The bell rang and class began, with no time to explain his antics even if I could. I'm sure the class evaluators are still confused as to what happened. He was an outstanding student who later won an appointment to a military academy. A teacher knows they have actually made a good connection with students when the withdrawn young person takes the time and effort to communicate. There was a student who didn't speak more than three or four words all semester yet he did a good job and was socially accepted by everyone. It is my belief that I received as much support and motivation from students as I was able to provide to them. How many jobs can you personally feel good about helping others?

The spring of the school year is always a time of dreaming of summer plans and reflection on the events of the school year. Teachers are anxious to feel the sunshine and submit to student pleas to have class on the grassy areas around the building. Watching students drifting around outside, I could hear a buzzing sound, and then a loud scream from a student near the window. Most old school buildings were not designed to have windows with screens, and without air conditioning opening the windows was a daily ritual. The ultimate test of a teacher's control and ability to maintain attention comes when a bee or bird zooms into the classroom. As always, it helps if I remain confident and calm even though I'm really shaking with fear. A person can not catch or swat a wasp or bee easily due to the high ceilings and fast insect movement. Asking for the patience of biblical Job, I kept on presenting the lesson while praying for the insect to exit. Most of the time this works, but too often the bee swoops downward causing students to jump from their seats and run to a corner or door. A bird moves a lot faster, and flies without pauses so the chaos is heightened. At least with a bee or bird there is no vomit that has to be cleaned up from a sick student leaving a trail all the way to the door.

The end of the school year brings out a person's desire to be free, and students skipping class becomes contagious. There are demands to have class outside, and the only one focused on assignments and tests is the teacher. But the last day of school is magnified into a combination of a hard rock concert and a birthday party. Students always want a party and sometimes have one even without permission. Occasionally, the party carries over to the bus ride home when a squirt gun and water balloon fight causes the driver to pull over and restore order. An end of the year party in the local park can be fun. Students enjoy chasing each other and playing various games including a tug of war. I have participated in a lot of tugs and found myself on my face or butt. It is especially hilarious if the rope breaks with fifty students pulling as if their life depends on victory. Students were flying in all directions and landing on top of each other, but enjoying every minute.

Remember when I said prepare, prepare and then prepare some more? The good news is you will be confident presenting lessons and students will accept your leadership. However, the bad news is preparation never ends. A teacher would probably expect to spend the day prior to classes reading and reviewing, but why does it also have to include weekends and vacation? This is my time! I must keep reminding myself! Who is totally responsible for the direction and agenda of the classroom? A person can whine about the burden, but it still falls in the teacher's lap. There are professional curriculum advisors and guides, but only the teacher can implement them. Nothing comes easy until the lessons have been repeated four or five times. Adjustments must be made to correct glitches and identify methods to emphasize goals. I need to stay alert and take the time to locate materials related to my curriculum. It's hard to imagine all the places curriculum supplements can be located. Many magazines have pictures and articles which need to be analyzed for the sections appropriate for students. Teacher specialty stores have many displays and visual materials related to my subject areas. One of the best sources is companies specializing in teaching materials since they have catalogs and materials designed by teachers. I usually modify the lessons to suit my philosophy and goals. Consider my field trips with previous classes to locations which have free or inexpensive brochures and postures which can be utilized in my classroom. Taking a vacation trip to locations that enhance my knowledge and expertise is a high priority. In addition, I can acquire statues, books and media to make the classroom effect personal.

Speaking of vacation, it's good to remember, if I am going to succeed for the long term I need to pace myself. Since when have I used common sense? Teaching has become the mainstay of my life, and my vacation time will be dominated by classes and lesson enhancements. Some classes are required to maintain certification and others are selected for the dual purpose of advancement in salary and improving my skills. When not busy studying, and usually just after the end of the school term there is a need to make curriculum revisions. Waiting, two months to do these revisions means most of the important changes will be lost. I need to do this while it is fresh in what little mind I have left. Take the time to review all the folders with lessons to look for notes and stimuli for improvement revisions. An excellent source of ideas will come from dialog and observation with my fellow teachers. I try to be creative by redesigning and adapting the lesson to various methods.

I have always enjoyed books, and now I get paid for expanding my knowledge base. Some of my friends have work with boring tasks repeated in mindless fashion. I have never been bored at work. When teaching, the human interaction can be intensified by expanding my personal interest in the subject matter. I can now attend lectures, plays, movies related to what is related to my teaching. Vacation trips contribute to personal and professional growth, and are certainly enjoyable.

With my spouse, vacation travel has included at least a hundred museums, historical sites, national parks, battle sites, Presidential homes and other educational presentations. Speaking of the excitement of visiting military battle sites! We actually had our own Battle of Gettysburg. When entering the Park, which was very crowded, and we were late and tired. While driving into the park, I said, "Turn left?" My spouse said, "Right", so we went into heavy traffic, and a delay of thirty minutes as the revelation occurred to us the word "right" also means "correct." We also enjoyed camping in these scenic areas until it rained for a week straight creating mud up to our ankles at the campsite. Add to this, no campfire and a night time of a dripping tent. Eventually our canvass home was totally mildewed. And then there was the search for James Madison's Virginia home. After searching for over an hour I pulled into a gas station for directions. We drove for another hour only to find ourselves right where we had started. It's a good thing I learned a lot of patience from my teaching career.

www.ingramcontent.com/pod-product-compliance
Ingram Content Group UK Ltd.
Pitfield, Milton Keynes, MK11 3LW, UK
UKHW041933190726
13854UKWH00004B/1566

9 781257 851218